5 NEEDS YOUR CHILD MUST HAVE MET *at* HOME

Ron Hutchcraft

ZondervanPublishingHouse
Grand Rapids, Michigan

*A Division of HarperCollins*Publishers

5 Needs Your Child Must Have Met at Home
Copyright © 1994 by Ronald Hutchcraft
All rights reserved

Requests for information should be addressed to:
Zondervan Publishing House
Grand Rapids, Michigan 49530

Library of Congress Cataloging-in-Publication Data

Hutchcraft, Ron.
    Five needs your child must have met at home / Ron Hutchcraft.
        p.   cm.
    ISBN 0-310-47971-1 (pbk.)
    1. Children—Religious life. 2. Child rearing—Religious aspects—Christianity.
3. Parenting—Religious aspects—Christianity.   I. Title.
BV4571.2.H87   1995
248.8\45—dc20
                                                                    94–33433
                                                                    CIP

Edited by Lori Walburg
Cover design by Jeff Sharpton
Interior design by Sue Koppenol

Printed in the United States of America

94 95 96 97 98 99 00 01 02 /❖DH/ 10 9 8 7 6 5 4 3 2 1

To Lisa, Doug, and Brad—
God's priceless gifts to Karen and me.

Your life choices, your character,
and your "make a difference" lives have made this book possible.
You are the joy and great riches of our lives.

And, Lisa, thank you for finding in Rick a son for us
who has made us even richer.

My Special Thanks . . .
To Lisa,
for her commitment and skill in editing and upgrading this book.

To Mel and Darla,
for so lovingly providing the environment in which I could focus
on birthing this book.

To my sister-in-law, Valerie,
for showing us what unselfish means
as the "unsung hero" and enabling angel of our lives.

To my incomparable bride, Karen,
whose wisdom, selflessness, competence, and tender love
have shown me Jesus and shaped our family in His image.

A Note from Ron's Children

For the next couple hundred pages, you get to hear from our dad. For these few paragraphs, we want to present our side.

Although our parents have been extremely busy people and Dad traveled frequently, he and Mom always made us kids a high priority. We knew that, and we felt that. Whether it was "dates" out, hours of childhood music recitals, high-school football games, themed birthday parties, late-night talks, or simply rides to the store—these experiences are treasured memories. During those moments our parents were shaping who we are today.

Mom and Dad have said they're not perfect. Now that we're grown up, we've reminisced about some "parent techniques" that kind of flopped. Uh, Mom and Dad . . . remember your attempt to limit our TV viewing by using "TV pennies"? And we'll never forget when Mom and Dad got us stuck on an abandoned railroad embankment on one of our infamous "family adventures."

In our teens and early twenties, we avoided many pitfalls and problems through late-night talks with Mom and Dad. They always gave us honest, straight-forward answers to our tough questions. And they supported us with their prayers as well.

We all agree that our parents had some great creative ideas on how to raise us. We're glad Dad decided to write this book, and that he could share some of these ideas with you. Our dad has permission to peek into our family's life in hopes of enriching yours. We believe you will be encouraged by what he has to say.

Lisa, Doug, and Brad

Contents

Need #5:
Spiritual Reality

Marching Off the Map

Wherever I drive, my atlas is my best friend. My sense of direction isn't. I can find that street in Brooklyn or that town in North Carolina only because some map maker drew all the details.

If I had been a traveler in the first century B.C., I would have been in big trouble. Map making was, to say the least, an imprecise art form. In fact, the map makers would draw what they knew and, when they reached the unknown, they would simply draw dragons and monsters.

I was amused when I heard about a Roman commander of that era whose mission unexpectedly led him beyond what was mapped. Writing from "dragon-land," he sent an emissary back to Rome with this classic message: "Please send new orders. We have just marched off the map."

Every parent in this uncharted time has felt that he or she has marched off the map. The world your parents raised you in is no more. The morality, the economy, the environment of your childhood is only a memory. If you are raising a child today, you have just marched off the map!

It has never been more challenging to be a parent than it is today. Our kids didn't come with instructions. The world we are preparing them for doesn't come with a map; it is uncharted territory with harder and harder questions coming sooner and sooner. And every parent is frighteningly aware of the monsters and dragons just beyond our walls.

In a sense, this book holds "new orders" for parents who know we are "off the map." It holds the good news that parenting is possible, doable, and exciting. This book is about hope for a mom or dad in a turbulent world.

Now, if I were cracking this book, I would be asking, "Who does this guy think he is, telling me how to raise my family?" Actually, I'm not sure there are any experts on the family. Each family is unique, so you are probably the closest thing there is to an expert on your family.

I once heard about a man who wrote a book before he was married entitled *Everything You Need to Know About How to Raise Your Children*. Well, he got married and had a couple of young children. At that time, he wrote a booklet called "Some Suggestions on How to Raise Your Children." Then his children grew to be teenagers. That's when he wrote a paragraph on "Why No One Can Tell You How to Raise Your Children."

No, this book is not written by an expert. It is written by a dad with a heart full of deep concern over so many scarred children. It is written by a father who longs to offer encouragement and help to parents in the pressure cooker.

My perspective is shaped by three factors:

1. Lisa, Doug, and Brad

God blessed us with three challenging children who have taught me more than they will ever know. Twenty-five years of parenting them has shown me so much of what works and what doesn't. And they have now reached that age where they are telling us how we parented them. Their reflections on how we disciplined and loved and decided, and how we didn't sometimes, have made us laugh.

2. My window on so many other families

After thirty years of work with young people and their families, you begin to see patterns of effective and not-so-effective parenting. I have been privileged to be invited inside a lot of families over the years, to hear the hearts of both the children and the parents. I want you and your family to have the benefit of parents who have walked this road ahead of you.

3. The wisdom of a perfect Father

Yes, there is one, but only one. And he wrote a book! It's a best-seller. Actually, it's the best-selling book in history! Yes, the Bible. There is amazing insight in this old Book for parents without a map. I have drawn on some of this unchanging wisdom to help us find some stable answers amid ever-changing theories of parenting. After all, who should know more about the family than the One who invented the family?

This is not a book of theory; it is heavy on the "how to's." It is not about how you have been parenting, because we can't have any of the past to do over. It is about how you can make the most of the days you have left with your son or daughter, however many or few those days may be.

Those dragons and monsters aren't so scary, especially if you know your orders. In these chapters, we'll establish those orders and chart a course that will bring your precious child safely home.

1

The Key That Unlocks Parenting

1:00 A.M. I am very asleep. Until the phone next to our bed rings. It's a good thing the phone is on my wife's side of the bed, or I would probably dismiss the ring as a bad dream. My powers of denial are incredible after midnight. My wife, Karen, must be part angel. She can answer at 1:00 A.M. as pleasantly as if it were 1:00 P.M. As Karen answers cheerfully, I mutter one word in my pillow, "Lisa." Sure enough, the call is from our daughter. She is phoning from college, where there is no night or day. No, it isn't an emergency, Lisa just really comes to life late at night. At that hour, she usually has a choice between talking to the mommy or the mummy.

Actually, Lisa has always been a night person, winding up as I'm winding down. And if ever I should complain about that, my wife Karen gently reminds me, "It's your fault."

I guess she's right. When Lisa was a baby, I was a youth worker on the south side of Chicago. Since our clubs met at night, and almost every night, it was usually about 10:30 when I would finally get home. Karen had made a mother's choice—either put Lisa to bed early without seeing her daddy, or let her stay up and know who her daddy was.

So I would come home with adrenaline still pumping from the night's activities, and I would be greeted by a wide-eyed, wide-awake, ready-to-play baby girl. She was the "dessert" of my day. I would crawl after her, swing her in the air, and dance her on my stomach. She would shriek with delight, giggle up a storm, and communicate with every sound she knew. I wound her up late at night, and she was wound for life!

Which brings us to 1:00 A.M. calls from college. I was reaping then what I had sown twenty years before.

I've watched that "reaping thing" over and over through twenty-five years of parenting and thirty years of youth and family work. Day after day, for better or worse, a parent is sowing responses, reactions, and relationships. You and your child will reap for the rest of your lives the harvest of your eighteen years of programming their personalities.

Nobody told me that the day I carried that wiggling yellow blanket into our apartment for the first time. When I brought Lisa home from the hospital, no instruction book was attached. At work, Karen and I both had job descriptions that spelled out what we were supposed to do to succeed. Now, with a life to shape, there was no job description. And yet, in many ways, what we built into her was what she would be. Then God trusted us with two boys to "sow," too.

As Lisa grew, we would jokingly refer to her as our "camera" because she seemed to be recording everything. Actually, every child is a video camera, quietly storing experiences, conversations, expectations. They will be playing those back in their actions for the rest of their lives. And their cameras never miss a day!

Eric was starting to feel some of that. He was my neighbor on a recent plane flight. For most of the trip, he was talking excitedly about the booming computer business he had started and the response he was getting all over the world. After listening most of the trip, I just asked a simple question: "How does your wife feel about how much you have to travel?"

My neighbor was suddenly down-to-earth even though we were still airborne. He said, "It's been all right with her, but now we've got a brand-new son." Then, with his business exuberance changing to fatherly concern, Eric reflected, "Now having a son, that's a trip. I'm really scared. I don't know what it's going to mean to be a father."

Like all normal parents, the responsibility of it all was hitting him. Whether you are shaping the life of a baby, a child, a pre-teen, or a teenager, you want to do it right. Because most of what they will be, they will learn from you.

The responsibility of being a parent has always been there for you, for your parents, for their parents before them. What has changed is the risks.

Before this generation, children grew up in a world where most people agreed on what was right and what was wrong. Today their world does not even believe there *is* a right or wrong. When kids used to hear the word *aides*, they knew it referred to the people who helped out on the playground. Now kids know AIDS is a killer disease.

Until recently, everyone knew that safe sex meant you had a wedding ring. But today it means you just have a condom. Children used to be able to be innocent for the first eleven or twelve years of their life. Today the media makes it almost impossible to enter kindergarten innocent! Today's parent is fighting what psychologist Neil Postman calls "the disappearance of childhood."[1]

Alcohol and drug experimentation has moved from high school back through junior high school—and now into elementary school. It was tragic enough when suicide began to claim thousands of teenagers, but now kids are beginning to choose death before they even get to their teenage years.

Like a flood breaking through a Mississippi River levee, a torrent of darkness has breached the family walls that used to protect children. As a parent, you feel a deep-in-your-soul fear about the world your son or daughter must live in.

So the responsibility of shaping our children is compounded exponentially by the new risks we are preparing them to face. Depression, violence, racism, "alternative lifestyles," Satan set to music, the "normality" of immorality, the power of friends, the bombardment of media lies about life—it's enough to make your parent's heart very afraid.

Or very ready for some hope and some help.

TWO-LEGGED THERMOSTATS

"Our sons in their youth will be like well-nurtured plants, and our daughters will be like pillars carved to adorn a palace" (Psalm 144:12).

That's not just a nice poetic thought. It's a promise from the Inventor of the family, the Designer of your son or daughter. If you "well-nurture" your son, he will be like a healthy plant—rooted, strong, productive. If you skillfully "carve" your daughter's life, she will be like the pillar of a palace. This doesn't refer to her figure but to a young woman who is a work of art—royally beautiful, solidly dependable.

If you do a good job nurturing and beautifying, here's the promised payoff:

> Our barns will be filled with every kind of provision. . . .
> There will be no breaching of walls, no going into captivity,
> no cry of distress in our streets. (Psalm 144:13–14)

The world's best-selling book, the Bible, says you can raise your kids in such a way that your needs will be met, the walls around your family will remain intact, and no child of yours will be taken prisoner or be in trouble on the street.

Now that's encouraging. And since it's from the Bible, it's timeless. Changing cultures and pressures don't change the outcome of good parenting! So how can we "nurture" and "carve" the child entrusted to us?

I learned a little about that one very cold morning. I don't mind if it's cold *outside*, but forty degrees *inside* is totally unacceptable. I knew something was wrong as soon as I woke up that morning and noticed my nose felt like Lassie's. The cold nose was followed by cold feet as I invented a new dance on a bare floor. The thermometer told me the bad news that our house had gone igloo! One trip downstairs confirmed that we had a cold furnace to match my nose and the floor.

We called our friendly neighborhood furnace-fixer and turned on the kitchen stove to generate a little heat. I've found a few minutes of prayer and meditation at the beginning of the day is a helpful habit. So, needless to say, I sought the only warm place in the house for that quiet time. Here I am, sitting in front of the open stove door, head bowed, eyes closed. And, one by one, the children decide to get up and wander into the kitchen. My wife told me their reactions.

Brad, probably only two at the time, simply walked around me in his sleeper pajamas, looking confused. He was followed by four-year-old Doug, who blurted, "Mommy, why is Daddy praying to the stove?" Then along came six-year-old Lisa, who loudly intoned, "Oh, great stove, please keep us warm!"

I was really glad to see the repairman. His verdict was clear—the thermometer was at forty because the thermostat wasn't working. As soon as the thermostat was fixed, the thermometer brought us much better news.

That Arctic morning impressed me with the difference between a thermometer and a thermostat. A thermometer reflects the temperature, and a thermostat sets the temperature. Unfortunately, too many parents are thermometers, and they reflect the temperature set by their child at that moment—hot, cold, loud, moody, nice, nasty. That is reactive parenting, forever reacting to the changing moods and behaviors of someone one-third their age!

An effective parent is a thermostat. You are proactive, knowing your mission and staying steadily on that course. Thermostat moms and dads set the climate with each child at a consistent temperature.

And the mercurial climate of the culture around us doesn't affect a thermostatic parent. If you have a clear agenda for what you must do with your kids, no cultural heat wave, cold spell, flood, or drought will change the climate you set in your home.

If you're ready to stop being a thermometer and start being a thermostat, then you're ready for *the key that unlocks parenting!*

THE PIN AND THE PAIN

Children, whether they're six or sixteen, are all over the map emotionally. They're up, they're down; they're cooperative, they're defiant; they're noisy, they're withdrawn; they want you close, they want you far away.

If you're a parent, you live in constant chaos if you follow your child's attitudes and behavior. What you need is an agenda for parenting that frees you from your child's ups and downs and focuses you on the factors that really matter.

Most parents are constantly reacting to the deeds of their children. Hello, thermometer! The key that unlocks effective parenting can be summed up in one loaded sentence: *look beyond their deeds to their needs.*

Most of a child's deeds are the acting out of needs that are met or unmet. If you want to change the deed, meet the need that's fueling it.

I heard about a psychologist and his wife who decided they would risk taking their infant son out to dinner with them. It was a fashionable restaurant, but they had high chairs, and Mom had a plastic bag of Cheerios. That should get them through a nice dinner, right?

Wrong. The baby was fussy as they perused the menu, tuned up as they ordered, and cut loose as soon as the waiter escaped to the kitchen. The parents tried everything to quiet their son's crying. They fed him, tried to burp him, felt his cloth diaper to see if it was wet, held him, and jiggled him, but nothing worked. The baby's candlelight dinner serenade went on uninterrupted.

Frustrated with the unexplainable crying, the parents left early. Baby cried all the way home. It was not until they opened up his diaper at home that they found out what the real problem was—his diaper pin had been open all night and sticking him in the side. I would have been crying, too!

Underneath the crying was a need. The deed of crying would not change until the need of a pin in the side was taken care of.

As our children get older, they cry out in different ways—with their rebellion, their music or clothes, their choice of friends, their anger, their shutting down, their escaping. Our tendency as parents is to react to the "crying," which often comes out in behavior we don't like or understand. But usually there's a pin open somewhere in their heart!

A "Look Beyond Their Deeds to Their Needs" mentality focuses a mom or dad on closing the pin instead of just stopping the noise. It deals with the deeds but also stands back to ask, "Why is he acting this way? What's the need underneath?" This kind of thermostatic parenting goes beyond the symptom to the real problem.

This perspective opens up a whole new agenda for parenting by meeting the *five needs your child must have met at home*. If these needs are met at home, you will send your child out into the world secure and ready for anything. If these needs are not met by Mom

Dad, that child will go out searching and vulnerable into a world of predators.

These five needs are lifelong steering currents in our lives. Much of what you are today is a reflection of your own parents' success or failure in meeting these needs in you. Now it's your turn with a new generation. And it is never too early to work on these needs in your son or daughter's life, and never too late. Even when they are full-grown and have children of their own, they carry those needs.

Meeting these needs cannot be delegated to anyone else. No teacher or church or friend or program can take the place of a mom or dad. God established the family as the garden in which lives would grow and essential nurturing would happen. Other supportive people can supplement the soul-building love of a parent, but they cannot substitute for it.

So the day you carried your "wiggling blanket" home from the hospital, you were carrying a trust from God. The Bible describes a child as "a heritage from the LORD . . . a reward from him" (Psalm 127:3–4). That baby in your arms was not only a bundle of joy, but a bundle of needs. His or her needs for food and shelter and clothing are easy to see. Your child's heart-needs are not as easy to see, but they are just as critical to meet.

What about the days and the years that are already history? We can't have those back, and it's a waste of time to focus on what we cannot change. But the future is yet to be written. It is time to focus on making the most of the days we have left in their lives.

In 1993, experts said the Mississippi River defied its own history. Residents of river communities watched with growing horror the steady rise of the river as its swollen waters moved southward. Every available person joined the crews to fortify levees that were about to face their ultimate test. In too many cases, that feverish effort wasn't enough. The river was higher than anyone could have predicted, and her muddy mess overflowed and penetrated many levees.

Eventually, all eyes were on St. Louis, where the surging Mississippi and Missouri Rivers would converge. It was a national nail-biter as we all watched the record crest rise to challenge St. Louis's new levee. The city had built it to fifty-two feet, many feet higher than the river had ever gone. And they built it strong. It cost hundreds of millions of dollars.

The flood lost; the wall won. The Mississippi crested there at just under forty-nine feet, much higher than ever before, but under the great "St. Louis wall." They built their wall high, and it was worth it.

Every parent knows that the river runs high around the family today. Just look upriver and you'll see families and children who have been carried away in the flood. And you may hold your breath sometimes as the pressure hits your levee. But if you build your wall high and strong, the flood won't, as the ancient psalmist said, "breach your walls" (Psalm 144:14).

You "flood-proof" your son or daughter when you meet the deepest needs of their heart. That's the mission we are about to pursue together.

Need

#*1*

A Secure Self

2

The Masterpiece in Your Hands

There's a bare spot at one end of our backyard. That was home plate for many a Wiffle-ball game with our boys years ago. We killed the grass but built the boys.

Doug still remembers his first day out there with his plastic bat and that ventilated plastic ball. I know he remembers because he had to write about it for a college class, of all things. Doug's writing teacher asked the class to write a childhood memory as if they were that age.

So our son climbed into his mental time machine and traveled back to age five, when he learned to play Wiffle ball with his father. In five-year-old language, he told how he tried to follow all Daddy's instructions, and then got two strikes. Then, in words something like this, he remembered the big conversation at home plate:

> So Daddy stopped throwing to me. He came to me and told me what he told me before. Swing level—don't chop. Keep your eye on the ball. Keep your head like this. Keep your feet

like that. He said a lot of stuff, but it was hard to remember it all. But I did remember the last thing Daddy said: 'Dougie, I know you can do it. You're going to hit the next one.' And I did! Right over Daddy's head!

Yes, I plead guilty to overcoaching. But when asked to reenter one childhood memory, our son replayed a moment when a parent's encouragement made the difference!

And that often is the difference for a child, as is the absence of that encouragement. Our primary feelings of whether we are okay or not okay come from our mother and father. As adults, we are still carrying around the self-worth or self-worthless tapes our parents recorded in our hearts. Today, we are making tapes for our son or daughter to play back wherever they go.

If we are looking beyond their deeds to their needs, we won't have to look far for a need that drives much of what they do. The first of the five needs your child must have met at home is:

THE NEED FOR A SECURE SELF

In other words, your child was meant to head out into the world each day knowing he or she is unique and special. No one's opinion of them matters as much as Mom's and Dad's. And not many other people will help meet this need.

In school a child learns very quickly that it is cool to be cruel. Kids make sure that everybody knows he is "too something"— you're too smart or you're too dumb; too fat or too skinny; too short or too tall; too young or too old. And they measure you by all the important things—the right shoes, the right hair, the right pants, etc. It's like a shark tank, and your peers swarm around any weakness they can find.

It doesn't take long for children to begin to define themselves based on what's wrong with them. "I'm short. I have a big nose. I have funny hair. I stink at sports. I'm fat. I do bad in math." The negative tapes roll early and roll right into adulthood.

Meanwhile, back at the ranch, there's "the folks." What they communicate about the child is who the child will probably become. That's why children tend to become the names their parents call them. Call them lazy, and they will probably be lazy. Call them helpful or beautiful or smart, and they will probably prove you right.

All day long, all life long, people are acting out in their behavior how they feel about themselves on the inside. When you look at your son's or daughter's deeds, look for the need!

So, how can a parent meet a child's need for a secure self? The answer comes in three life-building messages you put on your child's life-tape.

Message # 1: Make Much of Your Strengths

Occasionally in a seminar I will ask parents to try a simple exercise: "Picture in your mind the child that causes you the most frustration or worry." This is easier if you have an only child. No decisions.

Then I ask the parents to take a minute and write down that child's five most satisfying strong points—five things that are just great about him or her. It's fun to watch what happens, especially if a mother and father are there together. Mom writes one or two strengths, then looks up to try to think of more.

Dad cheats. He's peeking at Mom's paper while she's searching the sky for more strong points. He then writes down his unoriginal ideas.

Next, we go to writing down that child's most frustrating or aggravating weak points. Suddenly, there's a flurry of activity as Mom and Dad write energetically. By the time I ask the question, "Which list was easier to make?" the answer is already obvious.

So often, we parents know more about what's wrong with our children than what's right. And so do they. If your son or daughter were to make a strength and weakness list, chances are they would find it much easier to list their negatives. That's the side of them that may be fueling how they act, how they communicate, and how they perform.

That's why it's so critical for a parent to help a child understand his or her strong points. The problem is that most of us didn't get the child we ordered. Someone says, "I ordered an athlete, and I got a scholar!" Or, "I ordered a scholar, and I got an artist." Or, "How did I get a mechanic? I ordered a musician!"

No, there was not a mix-up at the factory. You got exactly the one-of-a-kind person God created and entrusted to you! Your job as a parent is to hold up a mirror and let your children see the strengths God gave them, and not to try to hammer in to them the strengths you thought they should have.

When we think of pluses in a person, our first tendency is to think of things they *do* that are good. Actually, we should probably start with things they *are*. Our strengths come in two categories: personal abilities and personal qualities. The personal qualities are what make you uniquely you.

DIGGING UP THE BURIED TREASURE

You may have a child who is a good listener. Are you noticing that the phone is less and less for you and more and more for your son or daughter? Someone must think your child is a good listener, even if a phone-ectomy may be needed some day.

Now no one gets awards for this priceless "listen" quality. There's no pageant at Atlantic City where some singing host serenades a girl with, "There she is—Miss Listener!" No gold medals and national anthems for the listenathon. But who has had a greater impact on your life, some superstar or one person who really listened to you?

We know the qualities that really matter, but we neglect to recognize them in our children. This "always talking, never listening" world may desperately need a listening child like yours. Affirm that quality again and again!

Maybe you have a generous son or daughter. You live with one who instinctively shares and gives what he or she has for others. What a gift! Cheerlead for it!

How about a great sense of humor, maybe a little weird, but a great sense of humor? That should be affirmed, because it's a quality that can give so much joy, healing, and perspective.

Maybe the Heaven Factory sent you a child who is a leader. Now your "leader" may say, "No, I'm not vice-president or captain of anything." And you will answer, "All I know is when you do something, two or three other kids start doing it. Now if people are following you, doesn't that make you a leader?"

As you're looking for strengths to affirm in your child, you may not need to look any further than the smile they have. "You know, your smile just lights up a room. I love it when you smile!"

One quality that is priceless but often unaffirmed is what I call "people radar." It's that special sensitivity that enables a person to know what another person is feeling, to enter into their joy or pain and share it. Again, no awards for this one, but it is a gift with tremendous potential to change people's lives. If you've been given a son or daughter with that radar, keep talking about it.

Well, the list of positive personal qualities is longer than we can detail. Persistent, encouraging, industrious, helpful, resourceful, organized, imaginative—look for this kind of buried treasure in the child at your house!

One reason kids have such a short list of their good points is they only think of abilities. And basing your worth on your grades or your speed or your talent is a fragile foundation. What you have that no one can take away are those personal qualities that make you valuable for a lifetime.

Tragically, kids miss the strengths that really matter, and often because we as parents miss them. Our list of their pluses should begin with the good they *are* before the good they *do*.

Parents often miss these positive qualities because they are sometimes the flip side of a weakness that drives them crazy! Our baby, Brad (who can now give *me* piggyback rides), could induce parental sputtering with his ability to thoroughly organize an activity he had not yet asked us to approve. If he wanted to do something with friends, he wouldn't start with us. Instead, Brad would ask the kids, set up transportation there and back, arrange for adult supervision, plan the activity, and then bring us an airtight, kids-waiting-to-go request. Or was it an announcement?

At times, however, we didn't think the time or the people or the activity was such a great idea. Had we been asked up front, a no would have only involved Brad. Now we were looking at causing hurt feelings and embarrassment, and being the grinches who stole Friday night. So we would address the issue of pushing to get your own way and leaving your parents out of the process. Bad side of the coin.

It took us a little while to flip that coin and see what may already be obvious to you. Brad had the quality of being a great planner and organizer! While we needed to check the runaway side of that, we needed to affirm the treasure on the other side. Today, if I really needed a "mission impossible" done, I think I'd ask Brad to figure out a way!

Occasionally I'll hear a parent lament having "a strong-willed child." We've had three for three! (I like to say they take after their mother, but nobody buys it.) Yes, there is a negative side of that stubbornness. But Karen and I got to where we started thanking God for a strong will in our children. That's exactly what it requires to take a stand for what's right when the wrong is popular, and to swim against the stream.

Some of your child's greatest strengths may be hiding just under one of your frustrations with him or her. Not aggressive, but patient. Not very disciplined, but creative. Overly emotional, but great sensitivity to others. Rebellious, but unafraid to be different.

When Mom or Dad says, "I love this about you, honey" or "This is something very special in you, son," you can be sure the young recorder is running. "Make the most of your strengths" builds a secure self when it begins with the qualities that can make your child great.

OPENING THE TOOL KIT

Cheerleaders. That's what parents are supposed to be for their kids. Now, many a mother would no longer want to squeeze into one of those little outfits, and most fathers would at least have to shave their legs. But every parent can be a cheerleader in the sense of being your child's Chief Encourager, cheering for those strengths a child may minimize or miss. If you want to get a sweater with your "hero's" first initial on it and spell their name through a megaphone, that's up to you. You build that secure self-worth by digging out their buried treasure and their positive personal qualities. Then, you open their life toolkit when you encourage their personal abilities.

The ability in your son or daughter may be academic or athletic, musical or mechanical, communication or computers. Whatever the tools your child has been given, invest in them! It may not be the ability you had in mind, but go with the Creator's plans for your child. If you've got an artist, invest in paint and brushes. If you've got an athlete, sacrifice to get some equipment. Invest in lessons, show pride when they use their ability, and make the recital, the game, or the show top priority!

Sometimes a personal ability may be as buried as a personal quality. Jon came every week to a youth club I was running, and he said nothing. In fact, Jon was easy to miss and hard to converse with. One could easily assume that there was little or nothing going on inside this boy.

Finally, frustrated with one-way conversations, I said to Jon, "I know there are some deep feelings going on inside you. Everybody has a way of expressing what's inside—how do you do it?" He mumbled, "I write them." After digging deeper, I learned that Jon had been writing his feelings into poems for years. I asked him to bring some of his poems the next week, which he did.

As I read Jon's words, I realized what insight and creativity were hiding under a silent personality. He was a great writer! When I told him that, he was really touched. And I even saw him begin to open up a little.

When young people are shy, their life-tools may be buried deep in the tool box. A parent's job is to look for those hidden abilities and praise them out into the open.

Especially as children approach the self-conscious teenage years, they may be reluctant to try their abilities. The enemy here is comparison.

I have told a young person, "You have a nice voice"—only to hear back, "No, I'm a frog." I've told someone he or she is good-looking, only to be told, "No, I'm ugly." Kids with athletic ability will put themselves down as "klutzes." What's going on here?

What they're actually saying is, "I know someone who sings better, so I'm no good." Or there's someone better looking, so I'm not good looking, or there's someone more skilled in that sport, so I'm a loser. They're making the mistake of canceling out their ability by comparing themselves with someone who has more.

Well, just because there's someone better doesn't mean you're not good! There is always someone who has more of your ability, and always someone who would love to have as much of it as you do! The Bible perceptively says, "When they measure themselves by themselves and compare themselves with themselves, they are not wise" (2 Corinthians 10:12).

When we as parents compare our kids with anyone else, we are telling them, "No, you're not unique." It's bad enough when a child does the comparing, but it's devastating when a parent does it. It comes out in statements such as "Why can't you be like your brother?" or "Look at Jenny, she does!"

We parents are supposed to be celebrating the uniqueness of that son or daughter. Then a child can, again in the wise words of the Bible, "take pride in himself, without comparing himself to somebody else" (Galatians 6:4).

An ability is a gift from God. A parent's privilege and responsibility is to help a child unwrap that gift, appreciate that gift, develop that gift, and put that gift to work to light up our world.

ONLY MASTERPIECES

My visit to Paris had to include a trip to one of the world's most famous art museums, the Louvre. You can almost overdose on masterpieces as you spend the day with Michelangelos, Rembrandts, and Renoirs.

But the big moment was when I rounded a corner and saw a room protected by a guard and filled with people. As I entered the room, I saw a lady in black smiling at me—from a painting on the wall. There hung the legendary Mona Lisa. I strolled over for a closer look and noticed a signature on the corner of the canvas: "Leonardo da Vinci."

You can't buy that painting, because it's "priceless." And yet I bought the Mona Lisa for the equivalent of twenty-five cents that day! I have her safely tucked away in a drawer at home.

Well, actually, I bought a Mona Lisa postcard. But there she is—same black dress, same smile. Obviously, though, there's a world of difference. The one on the wall is the original, signed by the artist. The one in my drawer is a copy. Originals are priceless; copies are cheap.

As we tell our children to make much of their strengths, we are telling them, "You are a masterpiece! You are a one-of-a-kind original, unless you try to copy someone else. Then, you go for cheap."

A masterpiece original is signed by the artist. It is valuable because of who painted it. So is your son or daughter.

A prayer of King David captures the real basis for a secure self:

> O LORD, you have searched me and you know me. . . . You created my inmost being; you knit me together in my mother's womb. I praise you because I am fearfully and wonderfully made; your works are wonderful. . . . All the days ordained for me were written in your book before one of them came to be. How precious to me are your thoughts, O God! (Psalm 139:1; 13–17)

King David had profound abilities in music and writing. His military exploits were legendary. He was the best a man could be in his country—the king. And yet he did not look to any of those gifts or achievements for his deep sense of value. He looked to the One who made him.

This prayer traces the worth of a person all the way back to conception when God "knit me together" and "created my inmost being." Our value is intrinsic, built into us from the moment that egg and sperm came together to begin a new life. And no one can take that worth away. That is a secure self!

And that is the strong message we, as parents, can record on the life-tape of the child we have been given. "You are a masterpiece, my son, my daughter! God only does masterpieces." That sense of value is really something more than self-worth—it's God-worth, firmly rooted in our Creator, not in us.

What a message we have for our kids! We get to tell them who they really are—one-of-a-kind, handmade by God, originals.

And that sense of worth goes right to a child's throbbing heart-need for a secure self. Your child will never have to accept cheap substitutes or play the "please everybody" game.

If you are committed to celebrate your child's positive qualities and abilities, then you are ready for the other two life-building messages and the "Three Faces of Me."

You are ready to help your son or daughter live a masterpiece life. They should settle for nothing less. After all, they are signed by the Artist.

3

There Was No Mistake at the Factory

The lady in front of me sure wasn't enjoying the game. Karen and I were at a high-school football game. I was watching the game; she was watching the people. But this lady wasn't watching either; she was sitting on the edge of the bleacher, craning her neck to see something beyond the goal posts.

Since she was so considerate as to speak loud enough for us to hear, we gathered that her teenage son was in the end zone where a crowd of kids was congregated. Her face reflected concern as she commented to her friend: "Richie's wearing a gray jacket . . . it looks like he's talking to Pam . . . she's wearing a red jacket . . ."

Touchdowns, field goal attempts, crunching tackles right in front of us—nothing distracted this mother from the main event of the evening. She was worried about her son, close enough to see him a little, too far to really know what he was doing.

That's the position every parent is in eventually. We take our children to kindergarten and release them from our sight and supervision a little. Elementary school, birthday parties, and sleep-overs at someone else's house, a week at camp—with every year, they get farther from our sight. Then comes the teenage explosion of freedom and ultimately the final release into their adult future. Like the mother at that game, we watch them from an ever-increasing distance, feeling powerless to affect what goes on in that "end zone" away from us.

And with each release, something deep in a parent's soul asks, "Is he ready? Have I done enough to prepare her?" Karen and I have now had three of the "big leavings" as we have driven away from a college where we were leaving one of our children. Each time, we have turned to each other and said, in so many words, "Unfinished business." We couldn't believe the "at home" years were over so soon, and we had more we wanted to do to get them ready.

That's why you need to focus on the five needs your child must have met at home. If you can send your child out with a full tank emotionally, you can sit back and enjoy the game. You worry a lot less about what they're doing in the "end zone" when you know they aren't taking a basic unmet need there.

No need is more basic than the need for a secure self. Young men and women who know they are important, unique, and needed are less vulnerable to expensive compromises. Peer pressure does not enslave a young person who does not need the crowd to find an identity. When your parents have raised a "masterpiece" person, you carry your identity with you all the time. A strong sense of God-given worth is the best motivation to go for the best and to resist destructive choices.

Which brings us back to the messages we parents are leaving on our child's life-tape. That first message is to *make much of your strengths*. An effective parent helps a child focus on the personal qualities and abilities God has wired into him or her. But after the strengths come the "yeah buts"—"yeah, but what about the things that are wrong with me?" To fully understand your strengths, first you need to make sense of your weaknesses.

Message # 2: Make Sense of Your Weaknesses

It's time for "The Three Faces of Me." No, this is not trizo-phrenia, just a little chart that lays out the three building blocks that make people who they are. I suggest that each member of your family make his or her own chart. In fact, it could be an affirming experience for family members to help each other fill them out.

Column one is "My Strong Points." If a parent has been a good builder, this should be a child's longest list—all those qualities and abilities Mom or Dad has faithfully affirmed. At the top are these words: "Build on Them!" These are the parts of you that you were designed to build your life on.

But eventually, we all have to face that other side—our weaknesses. Tragically, many young people have built their lives on those instead. There's no secure self unless a child can make sense of his or her inadequacies.

Column two of your "Three Faces" is "The Weaknesses That I Cannot Change." A child walks into a room and says inwardly, "Everyone's looking at my nose." Or my hair or my hips or my height. We have a hard time not thinking about the weaknesses that are "original equipment." We're stuck with them.

I'm short. Apart from a miraculous reopening of my growth centers, I always will be short. If that's a weakness, it is one I cannot change. It is a little embarrassing when I'm scheduled to speak for a roomful of professional football players, and they have to locate me before they can introduce me. Just in case I should forget how close to the ground I am, there's a world of taller people out there who love to remind me.

The Three Faces of Me

My Strong Points *Build on Them!*	The Weaknesses I Cannot Change *Accept Them!*	The Weaknesses I Can Change *Work on Them!*
Personal Qualities	My nose	My moodiness
Generous	My hair	My weight
Enthusiastic	My singing voice	My impatience and quick temper
Good listener	My height	
Sensitive to what people are feeling		
Willing to help		
Good at solving problems		
Creative		
Personal Abilities		
Writing		
Able to remember what I read		
Play the piano		
Able to teach other people		
Able to organize projects		

The Three Faces of Me

My Strong Points	The Weaknesses I Cannot Change	The Weaknesses I Can Change
Build on Them!	*Accept Them!*	*Work on Them!*
Personal Qualities		
Personal Abilities		

Of course, I like to remind them of a study I saw several years ago. It compared famous short people (average 5' 8") with famous tall people (average over 6'). The report said that the short people lived on the average twelve years longer than the tall ones! I told a tall friend, "I may look up at you, but I may come to your funeral!" And he rebounded, "Yes, but at your height, who would want to live twelve years longer?"

Well, the battle continues as we try to deal with those weaknesses we cannot change. Adulthood gives a little perspective, but children can come to define themselves by one of these painful "shortfalls." The struggle may be over something a child is not— not coordinated, not musical, not mathematical, not mechanical, etc. In any case, it hurts, and it eats away at a secure self.

NO MISTAKE AT THE FACTORY

So a mom and dad need to help a child know what to put at the top of the "weaknesses I cannot change" list in life. The answer? *Accept them.* Why? Because our weaknesses are part of the plan.

Obviously, the same Creator who designed us from conception and who wired us with all those strengths could have given us different ears or vocal cords. But he didn't. Actually, it appears that we all have been made a blend of strong and weak. If there were markets where trait trades could be made, you'd have one person yelling, "I'll trade you my basketball ability for your 'smart in English'," while someone else was dealing hair for height. Everyone has traits they wish they could change, but they can't.

That's okay. It is our weak spots that make us sensitive and compassionate people! If it weren't for these struggles, we would be plaster statues, useless to everyone. But we learn to feel for other people through the soft spots in our armor. A sense of personal inadequacy not only helps us reach out, but up. Knowing we need resources outside ourselves, we may learn to tap into divine love and power. It's like the song little children learn in church:

> *Jesus loves me, this I know*
> *For the Bible tells me so.*
> *Little ones to him belong.*
> *They are weak, but he is strong.*

The things that make us feel little make us reach for Someone bigger. Paul was one of the great leaders and intellects of the first century, spearheading the early growth of Christianity. But he struggled with what he called a "thorn in my flesh" (2 Corinthians 12:7). While we do not know precisely what this pain was or what it did to him, we do know what it did *for* him.

> But he [God] said to me, "My grace is sufficient for you, for my power is made perfect in weakness." . . . When I am weak, then I am strong. (2 Corinthians 12:9–10)

That "weakness makes us strong" perspective is ammunition for parents helping children make sense of their weaknesses. Your negatives can be positives as they make you soft toward people's hurts and open to God's power.

You can begin to accept your "minuses" if you realize that you actually have all the pluses you need! Fish don't have wings, but they don't need them for what they have to do. Geese don't have fins and gills, but why would you want to swim south for the winter when you can fly?

When you put your list of unchangeable weaknesses next to your list of strengths, you should confidently conclude:

> What I need, I have.
> What I don't have, I don't need!

For me to do what I was put on earth to do, apparently I don't need to be musical. Some others do, but I don't. I don't need to be a great athlete (I wouldn't mind, but at least my sons gain confidence when they play me). Now I am thankful for the abilities and qualities I do have, and they are all a wise Creator thought I needed for my mission on earth.

So parents give a rich gift when they teach their children to accept the limitations they cannot change. There is only one great question that stands in the way for us parents:

Have we accepted our child's weaknesses?

They won't be able to accept them until we do. The ones that cannot be changed are part of the plan. We can break the spirit of a child when we try to push and shove her into the mold we had in mind. We're not the Creator; we're the nurturer of what Someone else created.

GROWING PLACES

In high school, I weighed 210 pounds. Since I was only 5' 8", I was corpulent. Okay, fat.

I asked the doctor if I had an overactive thyroid. He said I had an overactive fork. I suppose I could have prayed, "God, why did you make me fat?" But God didn't make me fat; *I* made me fat. That was a weakness I could change. And I did. That opens up column three in your "Three Faces of Me" chart, the weaknesses you can change. Your child's column one should have a long list of strengths to build a life on. Column two should list the weaknesses you cannot change. Those are the limitations you make sense of by accepting them. But over your son or daughter's list of weaknesses that can be changed go these words: Work on them. These become personal projects that you encourage your child to tackle, one at a time.

You can change your temper. You can change your weight. You can change your hairstyle or your negativism or your silence. Change is risky, and you need a lot of parental cheerleading. But few things increase a child's confidence more than winning over a weak spot.

The problem is that many kids never even make an effort to improve. Often, that is because Mom or Dad has not started by affirming that child's strengths. It is the promise of column one that gives a young person the incentive to tackle column three. *If I've got all that going for me, I think I'll work on some of the things that could hold me back*, a child thinks.

Our problem as parents is that we often ignore achievement and pump improvement. If a child comes home bearing a report card with four *B*'s and one *D*, what do we tend to focus on? "Four *B*'s? I'm proud of you. Tell me what it took for you to do so well in each subject!" Well, that would be nice. Unfortunately, we open with, "A *D*! You got a *D*!"

Why do we tend to focus on the *D*'s in our kids' lives rather than the *B*'s? We must be thinking, *He is already doing well in that area, so we don't need to talk about what's already okay. We have to talk about what's not working!* That might make some kind of sense, but it sure undermines a child's fragile confidence. So many young people have told me, "My parents never notice when I do something right. I'm never good enough for them. All we ever talk about is what I do wrong."

If the people you value don't value your strong points, you have little motivation to improve your weak points. We have all seen young people who seem to have given up on themselves. They let their grades go, their appearance, their personality. If they feel like they are worthless, they will make no effort to develop what they believe to be a hopeless cause.

But children whose parental cheerleaders have applauded their pluses will have the confidence to pursue their minuses. They won't improve because they were nagged or criticized into it. When they know they're a work of art, they're encouraged to clean off the dirt and get a quality frame.

As a parent, you are meeting a child's need for a secure self with these two consistent messages: *make much of your strengths* and *make sense of your weaknesses.* There is one more soul-building message for the life-tape inside your son or daughter.

Message # 3: Make a Difference with Your Life

Our children left for school each morning with their mother's gentle send-off and their father's curious challenge. "Go MAD!" I often boomed out the back door.

Before you close this book thinking I have encouraged insanity in my children (it might be the other way around), I need to explain that battle cry. M. A. D. stands for "Make a Difference." And that is exactly what I wanted our children to think about as they launched each new day. We are here to *make a difference.*

That sense of life mission is a powerful component in a confident child. Parents are responsible to instill in their children the sense that they have been uniquely designed and perfectly equipped to make a unique difference on this planet.

The Manufacturer's Manual (more commonly known as the Bible) conveys that sense of personal destiny when it says "we are God's workmanship, created in Christ Jesus, to do good works, which God prepared in advance for us to do" (Ephesians 2:10). We are not randomly connected molecules. We are not protoplasm with personalities, driven by survival and guided by our glands. We are divine "workmanships," skillfully designed for earth-missions that are uniquely ours.

There are more "self" words than ever, but many of them lead to a very small self—self-centered, self-focused, self-seeking, self-pity, self-satisfied. Young people today will, unless aimed differently by their parents, gravitate toward being self-absorbed people. But the more focused you are on your own feelings, wants, pain, and needs, the smaller you feel. I still remember the all-city athlete who told me, "I've built a world as big as I can make it, and it's too small to live in."

Our kids gain no sense of worth by just taking up space or living for themselves. As parents, we have the privilege of introducing them to the excitement and dignity of living to make a difference for others.

Cindy was in a youth club I ran several years ago. She was one of the most depressed teenage girls I had ever met. She would call two or three times a week and talk to my wife or me, always spilling out her problems and general discouragement. One night I said, "Cindy, I don't want you to call me next week." She was not very happy. I continued, "Instead I want you to think of some people in this town who might need you and do something to reach out to them."

"Like who?" she asked.

We agreed that the people at a senior citizens' facility were probably pretty lonely, too. She gave it a try. Those elderly people loved Cindy and begged her to come back.

That was the beginning of a new sense of worth for Cindy. She went back twice a week for the rest of high school, and then she began training to be a doctor. She didn't call much to talk about her problems anymore. She was too busy helping other people with theirs.

That's the difference making a difference can make. Once we have helped our children see the gifts God has given them, we must connect them to people who need them. That happens as we encourage them to think through who is the lonely or different kid in their class, and ways they can reach out. They "go MAD" when they go to school with the mission to make someone feel important today, stop the gossip, listen to someone's hurt, stand up for what is right.

Parents enlarge a child's world and worth when the family becomes others-oriented. My wife involved our daughter in making a food basket for an out-of-work family. Our whole family scoured the house for toys and clothes we could give to burned-out families for Christmas. We went together to reach out to the homeless downtown. Karen has tried to make our home a welcoming haven for people who needed a place to stay or unload emotionally. Together, we have discovered the truth of Jesus Christ's challenge that you find your life by giving it away (Luke 9:24).

That list of strong points children should build their lives on is not only for them—those strengths are their wiring to make a difference. So we parents send our children out to use whatever they're gifted with—a smile, a song, a sense of humor, an aptitude for science, a listening heart, an ability to write their feelings—to touch, encourage, and change lives.

NO PAPER PLATES

We have two kinds of meals at our house. Because our lives are on a fast track, we have some paper-plate meals. When we finish eating, we think nothing about throwing those paper plates away. No matter how broke we may have been, we never washed our paper plates or put them away for later. They're cheap. It doesn't matter what you do with them.

Sometimes we have a fine-china meal. We have these china plates we keep in this special cabinet in the dining room. Now, these plates are usually saved for special occasions, like Christmas, Thanksgiving, special guests, and my birthday. This may come as a surprise to you, but we do wash the china plates. We don't throw them away when we finish with them. In fact, we keep them in a special place for special purposes and take very good care of them. Of course. They're worth something.

Most kids today feel like paper plates—cheap, not worth much. And they know what to do with a paper plate. They're throwing themselves away. Kids can throw themselves away academically by failing in school, socially by choosing the wrong friends, chemically or alcoholically by escaping into substance abuse, and so on.

Behind the deeds are the needs. If you know a young person who is throwing himself or herself away, it's someone screaming, "I'm not worth much . . . this is all I can get . . . all I deserve. I'm choosing what I think I'm worth." Or they're sedating themselves so they don't have to feel anything for a little while.

Somebody forgot to tell them that they are fine china. God didn't make any paper plates—he made only fine china! When children know they are *that* kind of valuable, they tend to live like it. They save themselves for special purposes and know they are worth too much to ever throw away.

If you are a parent, you are the one to show them their infinite value—they are God's one-of-a-kind creation with powerful strengths, weaknesses that can make them even stronger, and the ability to make a difference in a self-centered world.

When your son or daughter is out of your sight, your gift will still be with them. They will, in moments of pressure and danger, hear the life-tape you planted in their heart: "Built by God, loved by us, too valuable to lose."

Need

$\#2$

Sexual Answers

4

Taming the Birds and the Bees

D ad starts coughing a lot, but he doesn't have a cold. He starts clearing his throat a lot. There's nothing there. Finally, he speaks.

"Uh, Son."

"Yeah, Dad."

"It's—it's time we had a talk."

"Uh huh."

"You see, Son . . . well, there are birds . . ."

"Yes, there are, Dad."

"Right. And there are these bees, see? I mean—cows have calves. Um, see . . . there are girls—"

"Are you okay, Dad?"

"All right. Son, it's time we—we had a talk about . . . sex."

"Sure, Dad. What do you want to know?"

Welcome to the modern version of the infamous "talk"—the talk many of us adults never got from our parents, and the talk many parents dread, some never have, and few feel equipped for.

While our kids may seem to know more than we ever knew, they face far more sexual pressure than most of us ever experienced.

Kids have always had sexual choices to make that are beyond their parents' control. But not so soon. Some researchers indicate that one out of five young people have had sex by the age of thirteen. Whatever the actual percentage, most parents know that the pressure to choose comes earlier than it ever has, and usually long before a child even knows who he or she is.

Most of us did not grow up bombarded with sex all day long. Today's kids grow up with music that is sexually explicit and videos that hammer sensual visual images into their brains along with the music. That is a powerful erotic combination. Little children watch ad after ad that uses sex to sell a product or a program, even if they watch only "good" programs. We parents were protected from erotic saturation by some societal taboos. Today the taboos are virtually gone, and you see eroticism on everything from magazine ads to prime-time TV.

In every generation, there have been teenagers who had sex outside of marriage, but they were aware of something called "right and wrong." Modern young people play on a field with no boundaries. They are raised on the "normality of immorality." Not long ago, a girl felt she had to explain why she wasn't a virgin, but today she has to explain why she still is one. If you're young, you are made to feel there is something wrong with you until you've "done it." The moral consensus that once protected generation after generation is gone, leaving a guy and girl with no law but what "feels good."

If kids are under greater pressure than ever, so are their parents. Mom and Dad will need a lot more than "the talk" to prepare their son or daughter to navigate these moral rapids. And the monster of AIDS now fuels the fears of every parent. Our kids can get pregnant, our kids can get sexually transmitted diseases, and now they can die from sex. It's a scary world for a mother or a father.

One mom spilled her fears in a *Newsweek* letter to the editor. After describing herself as "a forty-five-year-old who feels battle-weary and apprehensive about the future," she said:

> What with the social changes of the last twenty-five years, we baby boomers need all the encouragement we can get. I was once a San Francisco hippie who believed she could help bring about a spiritual revolution. What happened? The economy turned vicious; AIDS struck and spread; families broke up in record numbers. It's hard to think much about your spiritual life when you're struggling to pay the mortgage and when your only prayer is that your teenager is practicing safe sex.[1]

Such a letter would have been inconceivable only a few years ago. There is almost a note of surrender in it, as if there is little a parent can do to help a child live in a culture where sex is out of control.

On the contrary, there is much that only a parent can do. And it has never been more critical that a parent does it. Others might be able to teach our kids the "plumbing," but it is in the warmth and love of home that they will learn the meaning and treasure of their sexuality.

Too many young people are self-destructing sexually because someone didn't do a parent's job at home. Remember, a child's deeds come from their needs, and usually it's one of the needs kids were supposed to have met at home. Certainly, preparing them to understand, value, and manage their sexuality must be one of them. The second need Mom and Dad must meet is:

YOUR CHILD'S NEED FOR SEXUAL ANSWERS

Even if your parents failed you in this area, you cannot afford to fail your child. The pressure and the risks are just too great.

It will certainly take more than Dad's infamous blush-and-dodge "talk." Meeting this need will require parents to outfit children with four moral weapons.

Weapon # 1: A Climate of Openness

During a break at a parenting conference, Maureen told me about a recent conversation initiated by her eight-year-old son. She was shocked when she heard little Joel ask, "Mommy, what's a whore?" Maureen managed to swallow her shock, but she said she also failed to ask, "What do *you* think it is?"

Mom agonized inside that a child so young lived in a world that exposed him to such trash so soon. She reluctantly plowed ahead, explaining in eight-year-old language the perversion of prostitution. Joel was appropriately wide-eyed during the whole sordid recitation.

Only when Mom was finished did Joel respond, "Do you know what I thought it was? A scary movie!" I guess I'd rather explain "horror" anytime.

Now, Maureen probably should have asked a question or two, but she had the right attitude. Her son can ask her honest questions, and he probably knows he will get an honest answer, even if it's for a question he didn't ask!

A parent's first weapon for morally outfitting a child is *a climate of openness*. If children are going to have the need for sexual answers met at home, they have to know it's all right to talk about it there. And parents are constantly broadcasting signals either that sex is an okay or not-okay subject in their house.

We tend to copy our parents when it comes to talking about sex with our children. If they didn't, we don't. But when we are silent, we allow others to meet our child's need for sexual answers. And who knows what those others will tell them in health class, in the locker room, or in pornographic magazines. That primary sexual curiosity that each child has should be fundamentally answered at home.

So how does a parent provide a climate of openness? First, give correct information. From the early days of a child's self-discovery, we parents should give factual answers about sexuality as we would about any other subject. Of course, you only give the information that is necessary and appropriate for that age, but what you do give is accurate. If we suddenly get evasive and "weird" when the subject is sex, we are sending a message that this subject is not welcome here.

Correct information probably starts with correct names for your child's anatomy. What do we communicate when we say to our child, "This is your chest . . . this is your stomach . . . uh, that is your—(*weird voice*) oogieboogiewoogie." Body parts have proper names, including the parts we may be embarrassed to talk about. If you choke on the right words, you telegraph a climate of closedness! Words such as *vagina*, *penis*, and *intercourse* are not dirty words (even if you feel like you just hit a reading pothole seeing them in this sentence).

Eventually, little minds will ask questions they don't know are loaded. A question about where babies come from or what a new word means is no different for a child than a question about the stars or the snow. A child only learns it's different if Mom or Dad treats it differently. It's all part of a little mind trying to understand the many creations of God.

Take a lesson from Maureen, the mother trying to explain "whore" to a boy who didn't want to know that yet. Ask questions before you answer a child's question. "What do you think it is? What made you think about that?" Once you've clarified what your son or daughter wants to know, answer it honestly, checking to see, "Do you understand? What other questions do you have?" Actually, the "talk" is many talks, unfolding sexual answers over years rather than dropping a "facts of life bomb" all at once. Your child will hear a lot of wrong sexual information floating around locker rooms, classrooms, and friends' rooms. You are building their confidence and equipping them to lead when they have the facts from the place these facts should come from—their parents. Our own kids would occasionally find themselves correcting a peer's misconception with the "authoritative" word from Mom or Dad.

A climate of openness means not only correct information, but also coed information. There are insights about sex that a boy can learn best from his mother, and that a girl can learn best from her father. Usually, if there is any information given at all, it comes from the parent of the same sex. Fathers with daughters are especially glad to leave the sexual subjects to Mom. But men and women are so different in their feelings and struggles in this area that a child is only getting half the story from one parent.

This raises an issue that will come up in many minds as we learn how to meet our children's needs—what about a single parent? The area of coed sexual training in the home is obviously harder in a single-parent situation. If the father or mother is unable or unwilling to participate, the single parent may ask a relative or pastor to help with the coed part.

The purpose of this book is to provide a focused agenda for parenting, one which frees a parent from riding a child's behavioral roller coaster. It is not meant to add burdens to any mom or dad who is already staggering under the responsibility. Rather, it is my hope that the five-needs focus will clarify and simplify a parent's task, single or not. Single parents are carrying a heavy load, frustrated by their lack of time to do what they know their kids need. Daily working on a child's needs, maintaining that emotional fuel tank, is actually a parental time-saver. It takes far less time to meet their needs than to solve the problems that result when these needs are not met. For reference, a later appendix is addressed exclusively to the challenges of single parenting. What matters most in this area is that a child get the whole picture of sexuality, male and female, even if only one parent can provide it.

Many teenagers go farther physically than they ever thought they would because they did not understand the other person's sexuality. He thought she was moving at the same speed physically that he was and ready to do more. She thought he was at the same slower pace she was, and suddenly things were out of control. Male and female paces are different when it comes to sexual passion, and both need to understand that.

Many young women are naive about the messages they are sending by what they wear and how they move. A man could explain that best. Many young men don't understand what triggers passion in a woman or that real men conquer themselves, not women. A woman ought to be telling him that.

Dad's the best one to explain to a daughter how guys talk about what they do with girls, how much it means to marry a virgin, how guys give "love" to get sex. Mom's the best one to explain to a son how much it means for a guy to be a moral leader, the meaninglessness of sex without commitment, the beauty of relationships without regrets. In the absence of Mom or Dad's input, a wise parent will still help a child understand both male and female sexuality.

SOMEBODY'S GOT TO START IT

A climate of openness is established by giving correct information, coed information, and by taking the initiative.

I still smile when I think of that mother who told me once, "I guess I'm lucky. My son's sixteen, and he's just not interested in sex at all." There may not be any such sixteen-year-old boy in the Western Hemisphere. What's more likely is that she hoped he wasn't interested and maybe that he'd better not be interested. But the sexual bombardment is so pervasive and so persuasive that no child can escape it. No parent can escape the responsibility to provide sexual answers. And if you wait for them to ask, you may wait dangerously long.

Mom and Dad should be taking the initiative to open up the subject of sex, to let Mike or Michelle know it's an okay subject around here. One way is to tell your child about your own curiosity about sex when you were young. Maybe you remember some misconceptions, questions, or struggles you had. A couple of stories of you-in-puberty should be good for laughs and for breaking the ice.

Stories of your courtship are always intriguing to the children who resulted from it. You don't have to expose all the gory details, but you can let them know that you understand romantic rushes and sexual temptation. Again, you have another chance to say, "If you ever need to talk about any of this, remember you're talking to someone who hasn't forgotten how it feels."

There are some books that provide an excellent starting point for open conversation about sex. Some parents have just handed a child a book and hoped that would do it, but a book is only effective if there is a parent attached to it. Concordia Publishing Company, for example, offers an age-graded series of books on human sexuality that range from early childhood issues through the teenage years. One dad just told me recently, "We went through that whole series with our kids, and it provided a natural way to start talking about subjects I otherwise wouldn't have known how to bring up."

Sometimes there are teachable moments from a TV scene, ad, or joke. Even though our family has carefully monitored our media menu, unhealthy sexual attitudes or actions can pop up. We have tried to use that as a springboard to ask questions such as: "What do you think that is saying about sex or marriage? What are they trying to get us to believe? Can you think of a good reason we shouldn't watch that?" Don't cut off their comments by immediately volunteering yours. We can turn the media negatives into positives if we use them to open up healthy moral discussion.

You can also take the initiative with the time-honored parents' lead-in, "What do other kids at school feel about it?" The subject may be virginity, homosexuality, a Hollywood scandal, or anything related to sex, love, and marriage. Often, a young person may be reticent about telling a parent what his or her opinion is, but the subject can be opened by the "other kids" approach. Just tell your children you're so old that you went to school with Fred Flintstone, and you really would like to know what's going on today. They will respond to the cry of ancients for up-to-date information.

Maybe you're a parent who says, "I know times have changed, and I ought to do more to help them in the area of sex. But this is really hard for me." In fact, you probably wish this chapter would go away, or that there were only four needs your child must have met at home. You know the need, but your inhibitions make it very difficult.

Tell your son or daughter that. Just being honest about your inhibitions can open up a channel of communication. "You know, my parents never talked to me much about sex, and I had plenty of questions. Maybe because they didn't, it's hard for me to talk about it. But I want to learn to. Sex is something beautiful when it's right . . . it's not dirty. So, I may turn a couple of colors or develop a temporary stutter, but I want you to know and have what I didn't have—a parent who helps you get the answers you deserve to have."

When you share your heart like that, you have recycled your inhibitions into openness. And your child has the green light to include you in his struggle for sexual identity.

Information and initiative—those are the bridges you build into a part of your child's life where a parent is so needed, and so often unreachable. Sexual answers were meant to come from Mom and Dad.

Sooner or later, you watch your too-soon-grown son drive off with a girl, or your once-little girl head off into the night with a boy who, of course, is not as good as she deserves. You might like to go along, but you can't.

But the sexual answers you have planted in them can go with them. That's why it's worth the struggle to get them ready. You can rest a lot easier when you know you have armed your child with four moral weapons, beginning with a climate of openness. The next three will build on that foundation of communication.

The need for sexual answers is definitely a "PG" matter—parental guidance is the difference.

5

Raising
"Sex at Its Best" Kids

O ur friend Dave may have been born too late. A century
ago he could have been the skipper of a great sailing ship.
But being born in the twentieth century, he's a suburban
businessman who spends as much time as possible on his forty-
two-foot sailboat. Dave is my idea of the ultimate skipper. Besides
the look of a sea captain, he has the instincts. When I'm aboard his
boat, I'm totally relaxed with him at the helm. Actually, I'm totally
collapsed and sound asleep.

Having grown up on Long Island Sound near New York City,
my favorite sailor knows the waves, the wind, and the weather like
old friends. Whatever the direction or the velocity of the wind,
Dave knows how to position his sail so we go where he wants us to
go, not where the wind wants to send us.

Watching the skipper skillfully capture the wind in his sail
brings back a rhyme my wife heard years ago. It says:

It's the set of the sail
Not the force of the gale
That determines the way we go.

You don't have to go the way the wind is blowing. That's great news for us parents who are sending children out into a stormy world. Especially since the moral winds seem to be blowing toward the rocks. A parent's job is not to stand on the dock fretting and fuming about the dangerous wind. It is to help a child set his or her sail to go the right direction.

That's why parents cannot be passive when it comes to filling a child's need for sexual answers. These are times for outfitting our children with the four moral weapons that keep them on course, no matter what the wind is doing.

A climate of openness is the first weapon, because it establishes communication on the subject of sex. With the lines open, Mom or Dad can deliver the rest of the arsenal.

Weapon # 2: Boundaries with Reasons

Kids used to adhere to morality just because it was right. Today that doesn't seem to be enough. They need to know it is smart.

Young hormones used to run inside boundaries most everyone agreed upon. Unfortunately, our children have to learn to manage their glands on a field where the boundaries have been erased. But Mom and Dad can help a child internalize moral boundaries, whether or not society reinforces them.

Tragically, the best "morality" our society can offer our young people is "safe sex." Society teaches that it doesn't matter what you do as long as you do it with a condom.

Well, let's imagine there's a wonderful five-year-old boy who is his parents' joy, except for one small problem. Johnny likes to play in the middle of the interstate! If he continues to play in the traffic, he probably won't see his next birthday. So Johnny's mother and father have an emergency summit conference with each other to discuss this emergency.

Mother says, "We have to do something!" And Father agrees, "You're right. There's obviously only one thing we can do. Give him a helmet!" Wait a minute! Did it ever occur to anyone that protection is not enough? We need to keep that boy out of the highway!

Maybe a condom is the best a values-neutral culture can come up with for our kids. But it's not the best a parent can do— we ought to be able to build a conviction in our kids. That conviction honors boundaries that have reasons, and boundaries that protect them from the emotional, relational, and spiritual consequences, not just the physical ones.

A thundering "thou shalt not" will probably not withstand the bombardment of "go for it." The key to sexually principled kids is a *positive morality*, backed by sensible reasons.

The promise of personal morality is summed up in the title of a talk I often give to teenagers—"Sex at Its Best." To be honest, that title makes some adults a little nervous. I presented this recently in a youth meeting where some parents had decided to come, too. Some were sitting in the front row. When I announced my subject (I guess they hadn't heard), these parents looked at one another with a mixture of shock, disapproval, and "how do I get out of this front row?" But by the end, they were cheering me on.

Teenagers are not nearly as nervous about the subject as some of their parents. I try to show them that sex saved for marriage is sex at its best. I present the reasons. Then I ask them to consider a commitment that is radical for people in their generation: "Beginning today, I will keep my body pure and sex special until my wedding night." They are surrounded by the people they want to impress and, in many cases, date. Yet, whether the group is scores or thousands, a minimum of sixty percent of them take that stand,

and usually eighty to ninety percent! Kids are ready to hear a positive morality and make it their own.

If you are a parent, your child wants some guidance, some authority on the subject of sex. That's why I believe we have to lead them back to the Inventor of sex. Jesus Christ made the Inventor's identity very clear when he simply said, "At the beginning of creation, God made them male and female" (Mark 10:6). If you want sex at its best, you follow the Inventor's blueprint.

Jesus explained the design:

> A man will leave his father and mother and be united to his wife, and the two will become one flesh [an intimate image of sexual intercourse]. So they are no longer two, but one. Therefore, what God has joined together, let man not separate. (Mark 10:7–9)

The Inventor of sex says in his Book that sex is designed for one man to enjoy with one woman inside a permanent, lifetime commitment. That is not the view of the Puritans or the Pope or the preachers or the Protestants—it is the Creator's design since the beginning of time. Sexual answers for our children begin by proclaiming, "The Inventor knows best!"

Our friend Mel has a garden to be proud of. And his family eats well from it. Fresh corn, melons, squash, beans, berries—and it is organized better than a lot of offices I've been in. Mel and his wife work hard to keep the weeds out, the rows straight, and the crops thriving. Of course, they have a fence around it. The fence is not there to keep people from enjoying the garden; the fence is there so the garden will remain one that people can enjoy.

That's why there is a divine fence around sex. It's called marriage. So, "marriage should be honored by all, and the marriage bed kept pure" (Hebrews 13:4). When a parent explains sex at its best, he or she should explain the marriage fence that keeps it beautiful. That is a positive morality.

There are animals who would like to share Mel's garden with him, but they wreck it in the process. The fence protects the garden from them. Children today are hearing about some of the "animals" that can destroy the specialness of sex. They hear a lot about AIDS and sexually transmitted diseases, and they should. Kids need to know that you don't just have sex with one person, but with all the other people that person has had sex with! That is not a worry if two people have waited for each other. Nor do celibate kids need to worry about pregnancy.

But those are the selective consequences of sex outside the marriage fence. Your child is probably not hearing anything about the universal consequences of making love before you've made the commitment. They are the other "animals" which devour the garden of love.

Kids need to know that they make memories when they make love, and that the memory of other premarital partners can corrupt the intimacy of sex with your lifetime partner. They also should hear about the bonding built into sex, that is "one-flesh" glue. Like a piece of tape stuck too many times, we lose a little of our "bond-ability" every time we "one flesh" outside the fence of marriage. So, sex beyond its created boundaries gives you memories you won't want and costs you bond-ability you will want.

Young people think sex will make them closer. It does inside the Inventor's plan. But outside of marriage, sex starts to put walls between two people—possessiveness, guilt, loss of respect, suspicion. Premaritally, a couple usually stops talking when they start sexing. Communication dwindles as the physical takes over, and the friendship takes a backseat.

Ultimately, when you remove the fence, the "animals" devour the specialness of sex that makes it exciting. Again, in the Designer's Manual, married love is described in these words, addressed to the husband:

> Rejoice in the wife of your youth . . . may her breasts satisfy
> you always. May you ever be captivated by her love.
> (Proverbs 5:18–19)

Someone might read that and say, "That's in the Bible! Isn't
that a little X-rated for God?" Not if he invented it! God is so for
the excitement of married love that he is against anything that
would ruin it—such as giving this unique love gift to anyone other
than your husband or wife! You can only have sex the first time,
one time. The thrill of sex at its best is for those who enjoy it
uniquely with one lifetime partner.

Thousands of young men and women have demonstrated to
me that they want love and sex at its best, and that they are willing
to commit themselves to boundaries with reasons. That should
give a mom or dad a new shot of hope! A positive morality is a
powerful weapon with which to outfit a child you love. We can
play offense on sexual morality rather than defense. "My son, my
daughter, sex at its best is worth sacrificing for. There's too much
to lose outside of marriage . . . and so much to gain by waiting!"

Weapon # 3: A Strategy for Winning

I have found an effective way to get all five members of our
family in one room at one time (no small accomplishment!). On
a cold winter night, I quietly turn down the thermostat and then
build a fire in our living room fireplace. Within the hour, one wife
and three children have each snuggled up by the fire reporting,
"Man, is it cold in here!" No one loves those fires more than our
son Brad.

But we've got a problem if I smell smoke upstairs. I would
call up to Brad, "What's that smoke I smell?" "Oh, I love our fires
so much," he replies, "that I decided to build a fire in my room."
Taking the stairs two at a time, I exclaim, "You don't have a fireplace in your room!"

When you keep the fire where it's supposed to be, you get warm. When you take it outside of the fireplace, you get burned. The fire of sexual passion is like that. That's why the Creator declares, "it is God's will . . . that you should avoid sexual immorality; that each of you should learn to control his own body" (1 Thessalonians 4:3–4). Keep it where it belongs, and you won't get burned.

I have, on several occasions, referred to biblical statements regarding the sexual answers for our kids. Obviously, the positive morality I propose we give our children needs some backup. These ideas need authority behind them if they are going to stand the test of conflicting moralities and intense pressures. While the positive morality should not be preached as a sermon to a child, it should carry more weight than just "my father or mother versus the world."

According to the Bible, sexual purity is more than just another social viewpoint—it is "God's will." Sex outside of marriage is much more than a physical or romantic act—it is a violation of the laws of God. Society has changed its mind about sex; the Creator has not. He does not determine what's right by opinion polls. When parents train their children to keep sex special, they must communicate that this is ultimately a matter of going with God or against him.

The challenge of Scripture is to "avoid" sex out of bounds and to "control" our bodies. That's a tall order for our children, living in a climate that is sexually out of control. As parents, we cannot just give them a *should*—we must also give them a *how*. How do you keep sex in the "fireplace" when so many of your peers are building fires in their room?

That is where the third moral weapon becomes important—the strategy for winning. When a young man or woman chooses to keep sex special, that cannot be a passive commitment. It involves several strengthening steps.

1. Major on friendship.

The American dating system pressures young people to become romantic couples before a boy's voice even settles down. Wise kids can see that this pressurized "dating game" produces a majority of marriages that do not last. There must be something better! It's called building friendships instead of pursuing romances. So many kids skip right over friendship and later don't know how to carry on the ultimate friendship, called marriage. As parents, we need to do everything we can to encourage coed groups doing things together rather than intense couple activities. Let your house be the place and your car be the wheels to facilitate guys and girls learning to talk, laugh, and share together.

2. Ask the right question.

It isn't, "How far can I go?" Instead, a better question is, "How much do I want to have left to give uniquely to my lifetime love?" Start there and work your way back down the physical ladder to draw your line.

3. Pace yourself.

Like a competitive runner saving reserves for the end of the race, pace yourself physically. The run to the wedding night is too long to use up most of your physical expressions too soon. So, our children need to know from us that they cannot set a line, walk on the edge of that line, and expect to stay inside the line. With several years to run pure, a young person needs to set "how far" a long way from the edge.

4. Decide in advance.

Glands make terrible decisions. We need to encourage our sons and daughters to set a high and firm standard before they are in a romantic situation . . . when their brain can decide.

5. Make each expression meaningful.

For some, holding hands or a good-night kiss are throwaway stuff, given carelessly. For a person who is committed to sex and love at its best, no expression on the "ladder of passion" is used up quickly. In today's sexual rush hour, young people rapidly use and devalue little languages of love that could have said so much.

My wife Karen remembers asking a girlfriend about a gold ring she wore. It had the engraving, "I. A. H." None of those letters matched this friend's initials. She was obviously glad Karen had asked. "It's a promise ring," the girl explained proudly. "The letters stand for, 'I am his.'" Since she had no boyfriend at the time, it was obviously a pledge for the future.

In recent years, Karen and I have been hearing about promise rings more and more, including recently when a couple told us about their son's and daughter's rings. These rings have no design or inscription—but they represent a promise. The ring is a token of the wearer's commitment to save his sexual love for his lifetime partner.

Kids who wear these promise rings look forward to their wedding night when they can hand that ring to their partner and say, "I've been saving this, and myself, for you." The kids who wear a promise ring, whether guys or girls, seem as proud as Karen's high-school friend was to tell what that ring means.

Virgin isn't weird—it's rare and valuable. We parents can raise moral leaders instead of moral losers when we fortify them with a positive morality and a strategy for winning.

Weapon #4: A Model Worth Waiting For

When I got really bored as a boy, I would buy one of those model airplane kits. Inside was a plastic bag filled with a lot of plastic parts. It's a good thing my father didn't insist on having a mechanical son, or he would have gone for a trade-in. But I laid the parts, the glue, and the diagram out in front of me, and I went to work on my own personal B–52.

There were moments when the diagram just didn't do it for me. I was stuck with a bomber wheel housing in one hand and a bomber without a wheel housing hole in the other. Something was wrong. That's when I went to my best source for bomber-building guidance, which was the picture on the box. There I found what the completed plane was supposed to look like and how the parts went together. It was hard to put the plane together without a picture of what I was working to build.

Our children need that when it comes to sexuality. We parents will tell them, "Wait for marriage." They will look at the one marriage they can watch and see if marriage looks like it's worth waiting for. Trying to put the moral pieces together is easier if they can "look at the picture" and see what they will have when they're finished.

Children need to see parents who still love each other, touch each other, find each other exciting. Society's propaganda portrays that all the physical excitement is either premarital or extramarital. We need to show them that it's marital. After providing an open climate, boundaries with reasons, and a strategy for winning, parents can bring it all to life with the fourth moral weapon—a model worth waiting for.

As parents, if your love is still going strong, let your kids see it and know it. If your love has cooled, the greatest gift you could give your kids is to get the "picture" fixed. If you won't work at it and seek help for your own sake, do it for the young hearts that are building their idea of marriage from yours.

If you are a single parent by death, you can still tell about the love of your life. And if you are a single parent by divorce, let the lessons of your tragedy be an example, too. As your child grows, share what made the good times good and the bad times bad. Let them know where the land mines are on the road to a marriage worth waiting for.

No matter where your marriage is on the happy/unhappy scale, tell your children, "Do it better than we've done it!" Any failures or mistakes of yours do not have to be repeated if you patiently show them how to make better choices than you did.

PLAYING OFFENSE

High-school football was a lot of sweat, pain, and work for our two sons. But they thought it was worth it. For one thing, they got to play for one of the best coaches in the state, and they experienced a lot of wins.

I don't think they would have stayed on the team, however, if their coach had started the season with this announcement: "Guys, we're going to make one little change this season. We're only going to play defense. I know you'll keep our opponents' scores low. No offense—we'll just concentrate on defense." So much for winning.

Moms and dads face some formidable opposition in raising children who are morally strong and sexually pure. It's easy to let your fears take over and just play defense. But that's no way to field moral winners.

If we let our fears prevail, we'll be silent about sex instead of open, we'll nag instead of guide, we'll create a rebel with our anxieties or accusations, we'll reproduce our own mistakes, and we'll repel with a negative morality rather than motivate with a positive morality.

Though the opposing team is big and loud, they should not intimidate the family where a child's need for sexual answers is being lovingly met. In fact, in the words of Franklin Roosevelt, we really do "have nothing to fear, but fear itself."

When you are building a child who wants sex to be special, the truth is on your side, the logic is on your side, the happiness is on your side, and God is on your side. You are taking the offensive—not just to survive, but to win.

Your child may be rare in a world of devalued love. But so is a vintage baseball card or antique. And ask any collector—rare is valuable.

Satisfying Love

6

Your Child's
Language of Love

Riverview Park was my Disney World when I was a kid. The old amusement park on Chicago's North Side was the place to go for thrills and chills. One day I thrilled and chilled a little too much. It was my father's fault.

Riverview had a notorious roller coaster called "The Bobs." The TV ads showed the parachute jump, the water slide, and the rotor. But the ads always ended with people screaming uncontrollably as "The Bobs" took the long plunge.

I thought about those screams when my dad said, "Let's try The Bobs." I know a boy is supposed to beg his father to go on the big roller coaster, but my survival instinct developed early. I put off the decision all day while we tilt-a-whirled and bumper-carred. Finally, we were at the end of the day, and I was at the end of stalling. Not wanting to be a wimp in front of Dad, I went for it, but under protest.

I don't remember much about the ride. Possibly a therapist could make me remember. My father told me about what happened. I gripped the bar and froze—in the middle of summer. I didn't scream, I didn't cry—I didn't do anything, including speak. My father kept yelling to me to see how I was doing, and I sat there white-faced, lips pressed shut, unable even to scream. My father couldn't enjoy the ride, wondering if his son was having the youngest cardiac arrest in park history. They didn't put me in the TV commercials. And that day one parent found it was no fun riding the roller coaster with his child.

Many parents have learned that it's oftentimes no fun to ride the emotional roller coaster their children are on. Growing up is an up-and-down experience. Your emotions are all over the place; your glands are transmitting confusion; you think your parents are heroes one day and zeroes the next; you're trying on identities and lifestyles to see which one looks best on you.

Meanwhile, Mom and Dad are watching with the same puzzlement and concern my father had on The Bobs that day: "What is going on in there?" Unless we have a clear sense of our parenting agenda, we will up-and-down, all-around with them. We're too often thermometers, reflecting their temperature, rather than thermostats, setting a consistent climate.

The key to being a proactive parent rather than a reactive parent is to *look beyond their deeds to their needs*. In that way you are treating the cause, not just the symptom. It's a way to get off the roller coaster. Instead of riding with their mood or behavior, you "thermostat" by asking, "What's the need behind this deed?" You can be quite sure it is one of the five needs your child must have met at home.

The need we explore next is one of the greatest sources of a child's emotional "roller coastering" in life. It is one of the most powerful driving forces on earth. There are ways in which only you, as mom or dad, can meet *your child's need for satisfying love*.

THE X-RAY QUESTION

You would understandably feel insulted if I were to ask you, "Do you love your child?" Most parents do, and you wouldn't be reading this book if you didn't love your child.

Your child's need for satisfying love forces us to consider what I call the X-Ray Question. The question exposes the inner condition that may help diagnose some of your child's actions. The question is: *Does your son or daughter feel loved by you?*

Thirty years of listening to kids have shown me that many of them are loved by their parents, but they don't *feel* loved by them. And the emotional effect on a child is much the same as not being loved. Love doesn't meet your heart-need unless you can feel it.

A child who is not sure he or she is loved is a ticking time bomb. Children who leave home without a tankful of satisfying love are vulnerable to the predators. It may be hard for you to read this without thinking about your own deep love-need, perhaps unmet by a parent who did not know how to meet it. Life becomes a revolving-door search for love in all the wrong places. Many an adult is still posturing and performing to get the love he or she should have gotten from Mom and Dad. The price is often high and the return disappointing.

Long after we are gone, wherever they go, our children will carry with them our satisfying or unsatisfying parental love. It is permanent emotional equipment. However happy or sad our own growing-up experiences, we cannot afford to miss on meeting this need for our children. Could it be that the deeds of your son or daughter are crying out, "Love me so I can feel it"?

Let me suggest an answer to the X-Ray Question. Your children probably feel loved by you *if you are loving them in their language.* Every member of your family has a personal language of love—expressions that really communicate love to that person. If our feelings for one another could somehow go directly from one heart to another, everyone would probably feel loved. But love in my heart is not enough; it has to be communicated, and it has to be communicated in each person's language of love.

I am an incurable romantic—the kind of guy who likes to send a special card or surprise flowers to my wife. Karen always enjoys and appreciates those gifts. But, like most women, she is also intensely practical.

We have this item called "garbage" in our house. Karen seems to feel loved when I remember to empty that garbage and get it out of the house sometime before the Board of Health comes. Over the years, her language of love has included such things as dirty diapers changed, dirty dishes cleared and rinsed, storm windows put in. Never demanded, not even suggested oftentimes—but her language of love. Frankly, I'm more into roses and cards than garbage and detergent. What makes Karen feel most loved is what I have the least of—time. Wouldn't you know, her language of love usually involves some sacrifice on my part.

That's the way it is with most people, including your child. As parents, we are loving our children in the ways that come naturally to us. But so often what they need is something it will cost us to give! Or it's something so different from what we need that we don't even think about giving it.

Our children's emotional tanks have to be filled with their grade of emotional fuel. And we parents must learn our child's language of love and learn how to speak it fluently. The alternative is a son or daughter who looks futilely elsewhere for love only we can give.

Tragically, too many parents are offering unsatisfying substitutes for the real thing. Like trinket love, for example. Trinket love basically says, "I can't be with you, but I'll buy you something." Kids will gladly take the trinkets and "toys" we buy, but those things will not convey love. The trinkets may be given out of love, but this generation simply does not feel love from things, especially if the thing is a substitute for an absentee parent.

Performance love is also love that does not communicate. It basically says, "Do well, and I will love you"—get good grades, have good friends, be a winner, don't embarrass me. Too many children have learned that love is to be earned. This counterfeit is given when you make me happy, and it is withdrawn when you do not. It does not convey that a parent loves you for you, but for what you can do for your parent. And that's not love.

One common counterfeit for satisfying love is triangular love. This occurs when Mom and Dad are not loving each other very much, so they direct all their love triangularly toward their children. That may sound like a good deal for the kids, but it does not work. The children want to know that the love they came from is still going strong.

Brad reminded us of that when he was still Pampered. Karen and I have been known to, as the kids say, "smooch" in the kitchen. One time we forgot that baby Brad was in his high chair, playing with a plastic clown we had stuck to the tray. As Karen and I were being romantic, we suddenly heard giggling and snorting behind us, enhanced by clapping and tray-pounding. We looked around to see Brad gleefully cheering on Romeo and Karen. Frankly, it's hard to kiss to laughter and applause.

But our baby was saying, "Go for it, Mom and Dad! I love it when you love each other!" I think everybody's baby feels that way, even when the baby is grown up. It has not been uncommon for Karen and me to be hugging in the kitchen, only to feel a little body wiggle between us. And there, peering up at us with wide blue eyes, would be Lisa, Doug, or Brad asking, "Can I be in the middle of your love?"

That is exactly where children are supposed to be. They are meant to get the overflow of Mom and Dad loving each other. Speaking of husbands and wives, the ancient Jewish prophet Malachi asks: "Has not the LORD made them one? In flesh and spirit they are his. And why one? Because he was seeking godly offspring" (Malachi 2:15). Healthy kids are the by-product of healthy marriages.

In a broken family, there is a love-deficit at this point. Acknowledging that, a child can still feel very loved. It is important that one parent not encourage a child to divorce the other parent, or for either parent to divorce the child. It is devastating to lose your parents' marriage, and it's more devastating to lose your parent, too. On the other side, single-parent love has to guard against possessiveness or indulgent love. We were never meant to "marry" a son or daughter. A single parent can, if he or she avoids the self-focus that divorce often spawns, very effectively give a child satisfying love.

Trinket love, triangular love, and performance love leave a child's emotional fuel gauge dangerously close to empty. If our children are going to feel loved, we need language study to learn how to understand the language of love that will get through. While each child is unique, there are six kinds of love that communicate to all children.

CHECKING THE STANDS FOR YOU

First, love that communicates is *there.*

Our son Doug had dreamed since first grade about playing in his first high-school football game. The day finally came, and his first game was away at another school. This was a freshman game, and the parental attendance was underwhelming. Karen and I were huddled conspicuously in the bleachers with a handful of other parents.

Finally, our freshman team came onto the field, walking proudly in their mix-and-match freshman uniforms. Of course, we were looking only for number 76. We didn't take our eyes off Doug. He, on the other hand, was all business, looking appropriately macho, staring straight ahead. He had waited a long time for this moment, and he was not about to be needing his Mommy and Daddy.

But he couldn't resist that glance. As unobtrusively as possible, he glanced from under that helmet into the stands. He looked until our eyes met, then quickly back at the field. No smile, no wave—except from us. But our son had to know we were there.

Throughout their growing-up years, children are constantly "checking the stands" to see if Mom and Dad are there when it counts. Your presence is a powerful language of love; your absence leaves a gaping hole. "I love you" and "good-bye" just don't go together very well.

Love that is there puts a priority on being present for the five golden moments in a child's day.

1. The Wakeup

It is important to have some parent-love in the first conscious moments of your day. Karen has always majored on waking up each child with a hug and a pleasant "good morning" rather than with a "wake up!" scream up the stairs.

2. The Sendoff

Horses, Olympians, and children run a good race when they get off to a good start. As often as possible, parents should be there for breakfast and a child's departure to school. Karen has prayed with them on days when there was particular apprehension and usually sent them off with her trademark launch, "Have a nice day with Jesus!"

3. The Reception

If you want to get a real reading on how the "game" went, be there when the "player" comes off the field. If your work schedule can possibly allow it, your parental presence when a child gets home will say, "I love you." Some days, children come in almost bursting with their day—hot feedback, too good to miss. After a little TV, play, or homework, their need to talk wears off, and you've missed the moment. A parent's job at the "reception" is mostly to hug, to listen without judgment, to notice your child is home, and to just be available.

4. The Debriefing

This may come right after The Reception. Kids need to debrief their day—not to be interrogated under a hot lightbulb, but to report, celebrate, evaluate, or explode. We always told our kids it was okay to let it out on your family, but not to take it out on them. Whenever you can love them by letting them unload their day, try to remember what their expectations were when they left that morning. You can learn a lot just by asking them to rate their day on a scale of one to ten.

5. The Happy Ending

If "all's well that ends well," it's good for a parent to be there at the end of the day. It's a time for an "I love you," an "I'm sorry," or a "thank you." The Bible's challenge to "not let the sun go down while you are still angry" (Ephesians 4:26) can be applied each night at bedtime with apologies and forgivings. At our house, we have tried to sign off with the Lord on our minds. The old parental encouragement to "say our prayers before you go to sleep" is still a good idea. An even better idea is for both the parent and the child to pray through the events of the day, especially giving thanks. It is better to go to sleep thinking about a Father in heaven than monsters in the closet.

These five golden moments are fixed points in a child's life on which a relationship can be built. The older they get, the tougher it gets. The busier you get, the tougher it gets. But the lonelier the world gets, the more important it gets. You won't make all five every day, but make it a priority to be there with them as much as you possibly can. The cumulative effect of your "there-ness" in those moments is a child's deep-down assurance that he or she is loved.

THE CAT'S NOT IN THE CRADLE FOR LONG

Love that is there also prioritizes being present for the important times in a child's life. It may be a concert, a game, a performance, or a parents' night at school. When I was little, I used to like to write stories. Every time I would finish a chapter, I was an author in search of an audience. And my mother was always willing. She would stop whatever she was doing to hear my dumb (adult perspective) little story. Those were important times for me, she knew it, and she was there for me.

Birthdays are a big deal when you're young (they're an accomplishment when you're older). A birthday is a "be there" time for Mom and Dad. So is a sick time, a hospital time, a sad time, a scary time. When you're a child struggling with a subject in school, you remember when your mom and dad are there for you.

There are usually certain activities that a son or daughter like to do with a mother or father. If it's fishing, make time to do it together. If it's reading, read. The "I'd like you there" activity may range from working on a car to throwing a ball to going to the mall to playing a board game. My sons' language of love was going to any field with any kind of ball, usually when my body just wanted to do nothing. Lisa wanted me to be there to read or tell a story with all the appropriate weird voices.

A lot of parents joke about getting a chauffeur uniform for all the driving they do for their kids. Actually, driving time can be golden time. If you use the time to talk, all those trips to music lessons, sports practice, the orthodontist, or school will help you build a relationship that's going places!

In a sense, our children are taking attendance. They are marking us "present" or "absent" in the moments and memories that matter to them. There is nothing a parent can promise or buy that will make up for a long list of "absents."

Ironically, the years our kids have the most time for us, we have the least time for them. We are so busy building our kingdom, our home, our income, our career, our security. And often we are doing it "for the children." We are doing it because we love them, but not in their language. They want *us!*

What a tragedy that so many men and women can work so hard for their family and have their family feel so unloved! This leads to a huge love-deficit in so many sons and daughters of busy people.

I have talked and listened to a lot of people nearing the end of their active lives. I have yet to have one man or woman tell me, "My one regret is that I didn't take more time for my business." I cannot count the times I have heard, "If only I had spent more time with my family . . ."

The time to set your priorities is while your children are still young. Many of our children would be willing to have less "stuff" if they could have more of us. "Better a meal of vegetables where there is love than a fattened calf with hatred" (Proverbs 15:17). That biblical image describes the ugly relationships in some beautiful homes, and the importance of building love over building material security.

Of all the six characteristics of satisfying love, being there is the foundation. A parent cannot continue to yell "I love you" from far away and expect it to reach a child. If you're not there, how can they feel your love? And if they cannot feel your love, it is the same for them as if you did not love them at all.

If you have missed the years when you should have been there more, it is never too late to tell your son or daughter you're sorry. It will help them to know that you wish you had been there, and that you want to make the most of the years you have left.

If you are still in the years when your family is together, capture each remaining day. Even if your child is mostly grown, he or she is in need of your love. There is a place in your child's heart that only you can fill.

As Harry Chapin said so powerfully in his "Cat's in the Cradle" song, our children have time when we have so little time to give them. And when we finally arrange our lives so that we have a little time, our son or daughter has no time for us. The cat's not in the cradle for long.

The years when they are taking "parent attendance" don't last long. The years when they need to feel our love are gone before we know it. Loving our children in their language really does mean making some sacrifices. But there is no price so high as a child who goes looking for love in all the wrong places.

Because they didn't find it in the right place.

7

Six Secrets of Love
Your Child Can Feel

I n Florida, Hurricane Andrew will be talked about for decades to come. It slammed into south Florida with uncommon fury, packing winds up to two hundred miles per hour. Those few hours of August 1992 left a trail of destruction that will mark a generation.

Some of that generation were in John Fulton's home, and actually, under John Fulton's home. In a matter of minutes, the hurricane reduced the house to rubble, with Fulton and nine relatives buried inside. One can only begin to imagine the terror.

"We thought we were going to die," John Fulton later reported. "So we just kept yelling that we loved each other."[1]

That is an amazing scene—uncontrollable fury swirling around this family, and they are making sure everyone knows he or she is loved. Maybe the Fultons have provided for all families a model of emotional survival.

Your family may never see a hurricane, but they are blown around by powerful winds of change and stress. Our child's world must seem, at times, to be out of control. During those hard times it's especially important to communicate clearly that we love each other.

For our children, there are six kinds of love they can feel. In the previous chapter, we saw that love that communicates is first of all love that is *there*. When you are present for the important moments in your child's day and the important events of his or her life, you lay the foundation for saying, "You are loved."

NO STRINGS ATTACHED

Life is a football game, and the stands are full. Your son or daughter (this is a "liberated" game) is carrying the ball. Your personal hero keeps advancing the ball as the crowd goes crazy. Now they are chanting, and it's your child's name. Then, on a do-or-die play, that kid with your last name suddenly fumbles the ball on the one-yard line!

This young winner-turned-loser looks forlornly up in those stands that had been erupting with cheers. Many are leaving in disgust; the rest are staring in stony silence. But wait! There are two people, still waving a pennant and yelling, if a little self-consciously, "Yeaaaaa!"

Who are these two wonderful people who do not desert you even when you drop the ball? Yes! They are your parents! And although you feel like a loser, you also feel like you're loved.

Love that communicates is unconditional. It is not given when you're winning and withdrawn when you're losing. Every child needs to know that he or she has in his or her parent a love with no strings attached.

The test of love is failure. Everybody loves you when you're doing well. But you find out who really loves you when there isn't much to love, like when you bring home bad grades or have a bad attitude. Children find out where they really stand when they embarrass their parents or rebel against their beliefs. Sometimes they seem to be asking, "Can you love me like this?" "Can you love me defiant?" "Can you love me sarcastic?" "Can you love me pregnant?" "Can you love me when I've broken your heart?"

If you can find the grace to say yes, you have given the highest love there is—unconditional love. That doesn't mean you pretend to love what they have *done*. You love *them*. Yes, you are still in the stands supporting them. But you will also probably come down on the field for a lesson in not dropping the ball.

Ironically, *when your children are the least lovable, they need your love the most*. When you feel the least like loving them, they will be able to feel your love the most.

The importance of this unconditional love is illustrated in what happened with Jim's long hair. Jim told this story to a friend of mine who inquired about his new short haircut. For months, Jim's trademark had been his shoulder-length hair. But his hair enraged his father. In fact, Dad had said, "You look like a girl, Son! You're embarrassing me and the whole family!" And Jim's hair grew longer as his father grew more distant.

"So did your father make you get your hair cut?" my friend asked Jim after the shock of seeing him with short hair.

"No," Jim replied, "I decided to get it cut." Then he told why. "A couple of nights ago, my father had a party at our house with all his important friends. I hid out upstairs in my room as usual. Suddenly, I hear my father calling me to come downstairs. He took me around and introduced me to all his friends—long hair and all! He even said he was proud of me."

"So why did you decide to get your hair cut?" my friend persisted.

Jim's answer said it all: "Because I don't need it anymore."

Probably without even knowing it himself, Jim had been saying with his aggravating hair, "Dad, can you love me like this?" For a while, his father flunked the test. But finally he got past the deed to the need and loved his son unconditionally. Once Jim knew his dad loved him, hair and all, he didn't need the hair anymore.

It does not take long for most parents to identify the issues in their children that make them hard to love sometimes. We parents are very aware of the traits or actions that hurt us, embarrass us, worry us, frustrate us, and yes, drive us crazy. Those very "unlovables" offer our best opportunity for proving that we love our children unconditionally. If you love them through this, will they automatically change as long-haired Jim did? Not always right away. And not always. But when people hit the wall and don't know where to turn, they almost always go back to the one who loved them through it all. Unconditional love usually wins.

That's part of what Jesus Christ was saying in what may be the most famous story He ever told—the story of the Prodigal Son. Jesus told about a young man who couldn't wait for the will; he asked his father for his share of the estate. The son used it to finance the ultimate party. He went to another country and blew it all on wine, women, and wild living. Hard times hit the country he was in, and party boy was cashless, homeless, and jobless. The only job he could find was feeding pigs for a local farmer. Jesus said the young man was so hungry that even the pig slop started to look good to him. This kid was a washout, a loser, a disaster! That's when the Prodigal Son finally woke up: "When he came to his senses, he said . . . 'I will set out and go back to my father'" (Luke 15:17–18).

The son was not expecting anything from his father—not in this condition. There was not one reason left for this father to love this son. Dressed in rags, smelling like pigs, life totally wrecked—the best this boy was hoping for was a menial job on his dad's farm. He had turned any dreams his father had for him into a nightmare. As Jesus relates the rest of the story, it is hard not to be moved . . .

> So he got up and went to his father. But while he was still a long way off, his father saw him and was filled with compassion for him. He ran to his son, threw his arms around him and kissed him. The son said to him, "Father, I have sinned

against heaven and against you. I am no longer worthy to be called your son." But the father said to his servants, "Quick! Bring the best robe and put it on him. Put a ring on his finger and sandals on his feet. . . . Let's have a feast and celebrate. For this son of mine was dead and is alive again; he was lost and is found." (Luke 15:20–24)

When a father sits waiting at the window for a son who has broken his heart, that's unconditional love. When a parent hugs a child who has just been with the pigs, that's unconditional love. When a mom and dad run to a child who has run away from them, that's unconditional love. That kind of love cannot always prevent a child's wandering, but it will almost always bring that child home.

I'm in that story Jesus told—all of us are. There's a prodigal in every heart, leaving the only perfect Father there is. In reality, Jesus was trying to show us how very much God loves us. Like the prodigal, we have spent our lives away from our heavenly Father, doing things that break His heart. Eventually, we get tired of the famine in our hearts, and we acknowledge our need for the Father we've tried to live without.

Recently, Jerry told me how being a father had made him acknowledge his own need. Jerry's a burly truck driver, a veteran of many a long haul. As you might expect, he's been an independent sort of man, tough enough to handle anything. But he was telling me, "I've turned my life over to Jesus Christ." I asked him why. Jerry said, "It wasn't because of some disaster—things were going well. But one day I was just looking out the window at my little girl, and I got to thinking about trying to be the father she needs—and I realized I'm not enough." It was his daughter's needs that made Jerry "get up and go to His Father."

An honest parent knows he or she is "not enough." That makes many of us ready to go to God and say, "Father, I have sinned against heaven and against you." That surrender is the beginning of winning.

Abraham Lincoln was not ashamed to say, "I have been driven many times upon my knees by the overwhelming conviction that I had nowhere else to go. My own wisdom and that of all about me was insufficient for the day." The needs of my children have often driven me to the same place.

Jesus' story answers a haunting question, "If I come to God after breaking His heart, how will He respond?" Again, in Jesus' own words: "He ran to his son, threw his arms around him, and kissed him." We don't get what we deserve from God—we are welcomed with unconditional love. Jesus should be the one to tell us this good news, and He made this reception possible by His death, paying for our rebellion from God so we don't have to.

Some days, maybe many days, moms and dads just don't have any unconditional love to give. They've been too hurt, too unappreciated, too wounded. It's hard to love someone repeatedly who doesn't love back or even seem to care.

That's why I'm glad there's a pipeline available to the only perfect Father. When we don't have any more love to give a son or daughter, He does. And He'll give it to us so we can give it to them.

LOVE WITH MY NAME ON IT

When you're in grade school, the teacher asks you to write little compositions on subjects such as "My Summer" or "My Pet." When you get to college, they start asking you to write about what went on in your family. Well, at least that's what our kids' professors assign. The students dredge up the memories, and the professor considers a career in blackmail.

Our daughter Lisa told me about one assignment where I came out okay. The subject was "Vivid Childhood Memories with

Your Parents." I was amazed as Lisa told me the first thing that came to her mind: "Dates with my father."

She reported on those nights (all too few, I think) when she and her dad would dress up and go out somewhere together. I'm not sure whether the significance of this event was "Time with My Father" or "Escape from My Brothers." But Lisa really remembers it. I would actually ask her out to dinner and try to give her some royal treatment. Sure, that restaurant was just a fast-food place to everyone else, but to us it was the Chateau de la Mac.

Why is that on top of Lisa's vivid memories list? "Because it was just us," she tells me. Similar conversations with our two sons yield similar memories. Apparently, kids need and remember the "just us" times in a special way.

That's where the third characteristic of "feelable" love comes in—love that is personalized. If you have an only child, that is easy. But as soon as there's more than one, there's a tendency to love the kids corporately: "I love you kids. You're one of my kids, so I love you." Being loved because you're in the "my kids" category is not very satisfying. In the crunch of endless demands, it is easy to forget that each child requires personalized love.

In our family, Lisa has needed Lisa-love; Doug has needed Doug-love; Brad has needed Brad-love. And they each have their own language of love. So you cannot answer a child's "Am I loved?" questions with group love.

One goal that can help is this: "I will give each member of my family all of me, at least once a day." If you're the old lady who lived in the shoe with "so many children she didn't know what to do," this may be "Mission Impossible." Even if you have fewer children, you probably will not hit that goal every day. But if you make it a goal, you may achieve it many days. This "just you and me" time doesn't always have to be long, just consistent. It may be just a few golden moments when you cuddle, debrief the day, drive a child somewhere, read together, pray together, or tackle an algebra problem. These personal moments have a cumulative effect of communicating personalized love.

In addition, a child needs what Lisa called "dates." The nature of these special times doing special things together will vary, depending on a child's age and sex. The combination of these more extended times together with daily moments of focused attention gives a child "love with my name on it." Unless a parent makes a conscious commitment to give each child individual loving, someone is going to get lost in the crowd.

WHO'S BEEN SITTING IN MY CHAIR?

In the childhood story of "Goldilocks," the three bears returned home to find that there had been an uninvited visitor in their home. Each one asked that question, "Who's been sitting in my chair?"

Sometimes the "bears" at your house may be asking a similar question: "Who's been sitting in my spot in my parent's life?" Children are very aware of the people, activities, and things that compete for their time with you—the intruders who are "sitting in their chair."

That is why love that communicates must also be love that is unrivaled. In other words, children feel loved whenever a parent chooses to be with them over something else that parent considers important.

If I asked your son or daughter, "What's your biggest rival for your parent's attention?" what would the answer be? The phone? Your work (especially the work you do at home)? Your hobby? Your exercise? Your friend? Your church work? The TV or the workshop? Every child is an expert on what is most likely to take their "chair" in your life. So you can imagine how loved children feel when Mom or Dad puts the rival aside to be with them.

Doug and Brad are more than brothers—they're friends. When Doug left for college, Brad experienced a role he had never had in his life. He was suddenly an only child. I did not realize how his needs had changed until my wife woke me up. Brad was coming home to a brotherless, sisterless house. And good old Dad was holed up in his study well into the evening, busier than ever with preparations for radio and speaking. If my study door is closed, the kids have always respected that as a signal not to bother Mr. Busy unless it was important.

Well, it was important, but Brad didn't bother. In a matter of weeks, Brad's language of love had changed. He needed more of a father's friendship than he had before. And Brad knew what his competition was—the study. So it became important for me to turn out the study light for a while and have it shut, with me on the outside. Brad and I had some great times, sometimes just watching a TV show, talking about the Knicks, or going to the mall. The issue wasn't what we did but that my son got me over his greatest rival for my time.

No, you should not make a big deal out of it: "Ahem. Please notice what I'm giving up tonight to be with you." Parents do not have to announce their "child over rival" choice. Kids have us under constant surveillance, and they know without our telling them when they have won the tug-of-war for our time. Just quietly skip the meeting or put down the work or let the project wait, and you are saying, "You are loved" very loudly.

LOVE ME, LOVE MY DOG

Love that communicates is love that is there, love that is unconditional, personalized, unrivaled—and love that is respectful.

For a few years, a parent is bigger than a child (be nice—their day is coming!). If you choose to, you can throw your weight around and treat a child as a second-class person. "Me big, you little. Me important, you dinky." You can do that, but you are missing a crucial ingredient in loving someone—love makes the other person feel important and respected, not insignificant and run over.

If children are going to feel loved, they also need to feel respected by their parents. It's like the old saying, "Love me—love my dog." Actually, our son Brad has taken that saying to literal lengths—he got a dog to help replace a Doug. I grew up in the city, where I never learned to appreciate pets, but Brad said he wanted to give me that opportunity. So dog Missy has joined us. I'm not thrilled, but I'm accepting. After all, I tell other people they must love their kids in their language of love. So I let Brad know how I feel about him by how I treat his dog.

The idea behind the "love my dog" statement goes far beyond four-legged friends. It involves two-legged friends, too. Children feel loved or unloved by the way their parents treat their friends. Parents can respond in one of three ways to their children's friends—put them down, pretend they're not there, or treat them special.

As his son approached thirteen, my friend Terry asked me, "What is the single most important thing we can do as parents to prepare him for adolescence?" I gave him my first thought, "Help him know how to choose the right friends. Friends will be the single greatest factor in the rest of his choices." Or, in the words of a much higher Authority: "He who walks with the wise grows wise, but a companion of fools suffers harm" (Proverbs 13:20).

You should not pick your friends based on who are the easiest friends to make (often they are the kids who are living for nothing) or the most influential (what makes you popular in high school is often what will cost you happiness for the rest of your life). You should choose your companions based on these two questions: "Where do I want to end up as a person?" and "Who is going in that direction?"

Unless your children are too wonderful for words, they will probably not bat .1000 on friend-choices. They will choose some you want to give your stamp and others you want to give your stomp. The older children get, the more their friends are almost literally a part of them. So how a parent treats a son or daughter's friend becomes a very delicate issue.

If you, as a parent, take either the attack or ignore option with your child's companions, you will reap two unacceptable consequences. First, you will send an "unlove you" message to your child by attacking or ignoring someone who he or she feels is part of them. "As you treat my friend, so you are treating me." Or, "love me, love my dog." Second, you will forfeit your ability to influence your child's attitude toward those friends. "If you don't give my friends a chance, what right do you have to criticize them?"

So teach your children how to choose the right friends. Then respect their right to choose by giving any friends they choose respectful treatment. Whether you judge those friends to be winners or losers, greet them, talk to them, feed them, drive them, get to know them. Every friend should feel important at your house.

If parents are uneasy about certain friends, it is essential they win the right to ask questions about those friends. Notice I said, "ask questions," not "pass judgments." Moms and dads win that right as they give each friend dignity and as they get to know those friends well enough to ask the right questions about them.

Above all else, it is vital that parents stay close to their kids in the years when it's so easy to let distance develop. A parent must never forfeit his or her responsibility to guide a child through the minefield of friend-choices. But he or she must carry out that responsibility in a way that brings closeness, not distance; that conveys respect, not disdain. Kids feel loved when you respect what and who matters to them.

There are other issues in loving kids by respecting them. For example, respect for privacy is important to children. They feel violated (as we adults do) when someone opens their mail, and respect-loved when parents leave that mail unopened. As a parent, you will probably lose more by opening that letter than you could ever gain.

A child's room is another area where he or she appreciates the respect of privacy. Knocking before you enter and letting children arrange their area as they want (within the bounds of appropriateness, of course) are examples of how parents can communicate dignity.

Of course, parents have the right to beat their chests and announce, "I pay for this house, including your room, kid. Everything that goes on here is my business." And they are powerful enough to prevail for a while. But the bill in alienation and resentment is just not worth it.

Music is another major factor for young people today. Like their friends, they really feel their music as being "part of me." When you, as a parent, attack their music, you are really attacking them. Again, parents have a responsibility to help their children choose constructive music. The questions are similar to those about friends: "What kind of person do I want to become? Is this music going that direction?" But bombing runs on their tapes and CDs will start a war you may not be able to win.

Having taught children how to make good choices, moms and dads should again respect their children's right to choose, especially as they get older. Parents can be responsible, show respect, and influence the choices by listening to some of the music, reading the lyrics, and discussing them. Again, a parent is saying, "I know your music is important to you, so that makes it important to me because you're important to me." You can agree to disagree but still leave them with the sense they are loved.

Beyond the specifics, love-by-respect calls parents to an attitude, a perspective on their children. It challenges parents to discard power-proving, child-shrinking approaches for a heart that looks for ways to dignify their children.

This respectful parenting is a strong ingredient in meeting a child's need for satisfying love.

DON'T MAKE ME GUESS

Three sons, and two were doing great. It was Brian, their middle child, that concerned Carl and Linda. Carl recounted to me how Brian had changed when he hit fourteen, commuting between defiant and withdrawn. It was getting worse, and Carl and his wife were baffled by Brian's worrisome and aggravating behavior.

That's when they called the Ma-and-Pa summit conference. They discussed Brian's problems at length. Then, out of the blue, Mom floated a possibility—"Do you think Brian knows we love him?"

Dad responded in typical fatherly fashion, "Of course he knows we love him. Why does he think I work so hard every day? He's got a room. He's got clothes. He's got plenty of food. He must know we love him."

Then Linda asked the knockout question, "How long has it been since we told him?"

Carl started to give an answer, then realized he didn't have one. "I can't remember," he said.

"Maybe he can't either," Linda concluded.

So Linda and Carl decided right there and then that they would start telling Brian they loved him.

They didn't have to wait long for the opportunity. Brian came shuffling in only minutes later. Asked "how was your night?" he responded with his usual Neanderthal grunt. He moved through the living room, past his parents, and up the stairs. Linda went to the bottom of the stairs and called up a few simple words: "Good night, Brian. Dad and I love you."

Suddenly a voice from upstairs asked, "What did you say?"

And this time Dad said it: "We love you, Brian."

"Oh" was all the response they got.

But Carl and Linda tell me that night, and more nights like it, literally began a turnaround in their son. They began to communicate their love, and the walls around their son came down. Like so many parents, Carl and Linda had assumed their child knew he was loved, but they hadn't *told* him.

As we conclude a strategy for loving children so they feel loved, we must add one final characteristic of that love—it must be expressed. It's so obvious that we often miss it. Too many families are conducted on the basis of "I love you until further notice." In other words, "I told you I love you a while back, and if I ever change my mind, you'll be the first to know."

That might work for the lover, but it doesn't work for the lovee. We all need regular, daily assurance of where we stand with the significant people in our lives. Husbands and wives need it from each other, and children desperately need it from their parents. As our children leave the cuddly stage, enter the awkward stage, then the impossible stage, they are not as easy to love. But that's when they need it most.

As kids grow and change, they are not even sure they love themselves. They are silently crying, "I'm not sure how other people feel about me, or how I feel about me. I need to know how you feel about me, Mom and Dad." So let's tell them.

It is a great goal to tell each child of our love and touch each child with our love at least once a day. "Have I told them today that I love them?" should be a parent's daily self-examination. Ask yourself, "Have I touched them in a way that demonstrates my love?" Obviously, the cuddle of childhood must be modified as kids grow older to age-appropriate expressions. While a parent will change the means of showing love physically, he or she must never change the commitment to show it.

When Brian's life took a tailspin, his parents went to the right place for answers. They looked beyond his deeds to his needs! And underneath the deeds they had been reacting to, they found a need they could act upon. Brian was crying for satisfying love.

Every child is asking for that love, no matter how old. Meeting that need is one of a parent's most life-shaping assignments. A love-hole in a human heart, left unfilled by a mom or dad, is a blueprint for heartbreak—for both the parent and the child. There is a need for "feelable" love that only a mother and father can meet. Almost certainly, it will require sacrifice to love a child in his or her language, but nothing approaching the sacrifice of a son or daughter who gets lost looking for love—a love that child should have found at home.

If you, as a parent, should find that you are not enough to meet all your child's needs for love, you may want to go where I have often been driven—to your knees. For in the unconditional, unlimited love of God in Jesus Christ, a parent can meet his or her own deep love hunger, and find more than enough to fill his child's heart, too.

In 1976 Lynette "Squeaky" Fromme exploded on to every front page in America. She had pushed her way through a crowd and had tried to kill the President of the United States. She was seventeen years old.

Investigators found her proud that she was a follower of Charles Manson. The world knows Manson as a crazed killer who worked through his small, dedicated band of fanatical "disciples."

News magazines began to dig into the background of this tragic young woman. Their reports found that Squeaky had felt like a misfit in her town, and so she wandered across the country until she reached California. There Charles Manson met her and promised to take care of her. She went with him and was willing to kill and die for him.

Reporters wanted to know, "Why would you give your life to a man like Manson?" I read her explanation in a magazine, and I have never been able to forget it. Squeaky explained that she had made a choice early in her teenage years. Here it is: "Whoever loves me first can have my life."

Someone probably had loved Squeaky, but she was ready to give her life to whomever made her *feel* loved first.

There are a lot of Squeakys, male and female. Whoever makes them feel loved first can have their lives.

For your son or daughter, be sure that person is you.

8

A Strategy
for a New Beginning

If I never have to move a piano again, that will be soon enough. It's almost as much fun as having a root canal. Our daughter Lisa had just gotten married, and Karen and I wanted to give the newlyweds our piano as a wedding present. The idea was heart-warming, but the process was painful. Sort of like your daughter getting married and her father getting to pay for it.

The piano is a baby grand, and it definitely takes a six-man operation to move it down the front steps, across the yard, and up into a truck. We covered it with blankets to avoid scarring, strapped it to a "skid board," and shouted, "Heave ho!" The challenge, of course, was the front steps, where the wheels did us little good. There I had a flashback to when I was a kid and my dad had a hernia operation. I was sure he had said something about moving a piano just before that.

Actually, six men could handle the load. The weight was not the major problem. Our greatest problem was summed up in the cries of two or three movers, asking from somewhere underneath that baby grand: "Where do I grab this thing?" We had a heavy load, and there were no handles with which we could grab it.

Many parents feel that way when it comes to the heavy task of meeting the five needs their child must have met at home. In fact, you may be feeling overwhelmed as you read about all you have to carry as a parent—showing the sensitivity it requires to build a secure self, having the courage and wisdom to provide sexual answers in a moral minefield, and knowing and "speaking" your children's language of satisfying love, whether they're lovable or not. And there are two more deep heart-needs that we have not even explored yet! P.S.—you have to continue to meet all your other responsibilities, too.

Feeling the weight, you have every right to yell, "Where do I grab this parenting agenda?" It's nice to know what your mission is supposed to be, but how do you do it all? Where do you start? Before we proceed any further into these five needs, we must take a "how-to" time-out. The purpose of this "meet the needs instead of react to the deeds" approach is to encourage parents, not bury them. And there is real hope in needs-based parenting if you know where to grab it.

Addiction recovery programs emphasize that "today is the first day of the rest of your life." That is a helpful perspective for a parent, too. You can't have the past back, and the future isn't here yet. So what we parents need, no matter what the ages of our children, is a strategy for a new beginning.

DON'T TOUCH "REPLAY"

When Doug and Brad played high-school football, the highlight of the week was the game on Saturday. The lowlight of the week was the game films on Monday. That was where the players got to watch their mistakes again and again. Coaches have this way of stopping the film right on your error, then rewinding and replaying it a couple of times until you (and everyone else) have memorized your mistake!

Every parent has made his or her share of mistakes in raising a child—too busy, too critical, too hard to please, too angry; not enough affection or discipline or listening or affirming. Obviously, you care about your children and how you are parenting them. Parents who don't care would not be reading this book. Because you care, an exploration of your child's needs will bring back memories of things you have done that you wish you hadn't, and things you should have done that you didn't. You may be replaying your mistakes over and over again, punishing yourself for hurtful actions or wasted opportunities.

But you can't have those back. Life does not allow for "do-overs." A new beginning means that you *put your past mistakes behind you.* No more replays.

It is healthy to recognize and acknowledge parenting mistakes, but not to dwell on them. Some mothers and fathers refuse to see themselves in the mirror of their child's needs and struggles. Not taking responsibility is the ultimate cowardice of all. Parents are the major shaping influence in children's lives by what they do and what they fail to do. So a healthy human being will replay the tape to see what needs fixing. But then that parent needs to focus on making it right, not drowning in guilt.

Mothers and fathers who focus on their failures will not be proactive parents. They will tend to just give up because "I've already messed up" or "It's too late." Or they will withdraw from a child who seems like a symbol of their failure, thus abandoning that child to a tragic and futile search for love.

So how can parents put past mistakes behind them? Address those mistakes honestly with the people who have been hurt by them! You can redeem the past by confessing shortcomings and asking forgiveness.

Jack almost waited too long. His "wakeup call" came from the emergency room at the local hospital. They told him that his teenage daughter Vicki had intentionally overdosed on pills and that they were trying to save her life. Standing by Vicki's bed, Jack prayed as he had never prayed in his life. Thankfully, his daughter survived.

Although any suicidal choice involves many factors, Jack stepped up to his share of the responsibility. Soon after that long night in the emergency room, he did one of the hardest things he had ever done—he admitted to his daughter where he had failed her. He asked for her forgiveness and for a chance to change. He got both, along with a new beginning in his relationship with the daughter he loved so much but who did not know it.

The "new beginning" conversation may go something like this:

"My son . . . my daughter, I want to ask you to forgive me. I really want the rest of our years to be the best of our years. But they can't be if I don't clean up some garbage from the past. I know I've hurt you by the ways I _____. And you have needed more _____ than I have given you. You have been raised by an imperfect parent, and so was I. Your child will be, too. But I want to deal with these weaknesses, and I need your forgiveness. In fact, I need your help, because it won't be easy to change a way I have been for a long time. I won't suddenly start being perfect, but I will get better and better. So I'll continue to need your forgiveness and help. But I want to make today a new beginning."

That kind of vulnerability has a lot of healing power. While you cannot go back and do what you should have done, you can let your son or daughter know that you wish you had and that you are committed to change. Dealing with the mistakes of the past is an important step in making today "the first day of the rest of your life."

It's hard to do. But not nearly as hard as a midnight call from the emergency room.

BITE-SIZED CHUNKS

It was a major milestone in our children's lives when they learned to feed themselves. No more "open your mouth, here comes the airplane" games. But when we put a piece of meat in front of them, they did need a little help from us. Knowing they could not handle a whole hamburger yet, we faithfully cut it into bite-sized chunks that they could handle.

Actually, parents need bite-sized chunks, too, as they try to digest parenting challenges that are too big to handle. When parents try to deal with all the problems and possibilities of the next few weeks, months, and years, fear and freezing set in. So, the second step in a strategy for a new beginning is simply, *have a good day.*

An effective parent lives in the present, not in the past or the future. When parents focus on the failures of the past, they are paralyzed by guilt. When they agonize over the possibilities of the future, they are paralyzed by fear. In either case, they miss the moment that is right in front of them. A new beginning in a family comes from focusing on what is today, not what should have been yesterday or might be tomorrow. As a parent, you need to relax and just try to make today a good day for your son or daughter.

It is hard to do that when you are worried about the future. A parent looks ahead and thinks, "If my child keeps going down this road, I know what disaster this can lead to." To a certain extent, moms and dads do need to help their children see where various roads lead, to draw out the lines and show how to evaluate the consequences of their decisions. That's wisdom. But it is worry that makes a parent freeze up or overreact.

Worry tries to drag tomorrow into today. That's why Jesus Christ advised us, "Do not worry about tomorrow, for tomorrow will worry about itself. Each day has enough trouble of its own" (Matthew 6:34). Worry leads to parenting from fear. And fearful parenting often produces the very things it feared:

- Parents become more lecturers than listeners.
- Children stop talking with their parents about the things their parents are obviously "hyper" about.
- Parents tend to keep "harping on" the danger areas, sometimes creating a rebel.
- Children feel distrusted by their parents: "They seem to think I'm the kind of person who could do those kinds of things—so what's the use?"
- Parents overreact to today's deeds, attaching to those deeds all the fears about where this could lead, and probably missing the needs behind the deeds.

The only perfect Father has a great word for us parents in His Book:

> God did not give us a spirit of timidity [or fear], but a spirit of power, of love, and of self-discipline. (2 Timothy 1:7)

No strategy for effective parenting can be based on fear of the future.

Positive parents follow the ancient Latin maxim, "*carpe diem*"—seize the day! They make these twenty-four hours their focus. Instead of being overwhelmed by meeting a life-need for a secure self, a mom or dad can simply ask questions such as:

- "Have I complimented my child today on a personal trait or a personal ability?"
- "Have I helped my child deal with any attacks or failures or criticism he or she experienced today?"

Instead of self-torture over whether or not a child feels loved enough, a "*carpe diem*" parent focuses on today and says:

- "Am I giving each child all of me at least once today (even if it's brief sometimes)?"
- "Have I told each child I love him or her today, and touched each one?"

- "Am I going to be there today for the thing that matters most to my son or daughter?"

With the five deepest needs as your agenda, you, as a parent, have the ingredients of a good day. Our kids don't experience life as months and years. Son Doug reminded us of that shortly after his mother turned forty. She handled that dreaded milestone totally unfazed—"just another birthday." But later Doug came along with this unsettling question, "Mom, do you realize you've been on earth for 14,663 days?" Forty years is one thing, but 14,663 days? Actually, children really do experience life that way—as days.

That is why parents must break down their child-building into twenty-four-hour, bite-sized chunks. They won't allow themselves to be sidetracked from need-meeting by analysis or paralysis, by guilt or anxiety. Positive mothers and fathers wake up in the morning determined simply to "have a good day."

A PAPER BRIDGE

The third step in the strategy for a new beginning is to *write a letter*. Writing a letter to a son or daughter can build a "paper bridge" over a growing chasm. It may actually turn out to be the first of several letters that will heal or grow a relationship.

"Why a letter?" is a legitimate question. The reasons are straight forward:

- A parent will say it better because there will be no interruptions or detours.
- A child will receive it better because he or she does not have to be thinking about how to answer or react.
- A letter can be revisited and considered many times—a conversation cannot.

"What should the letter say?" is a good question number two. Most of the content must come from the heart of a mom or dad, of course. But the paragraphs might begin with thoughts such as these:

- "I love you . . ."
- "I appreciate . . ."

This is an expression of the specific qualities, abilities, and actions you, as a parent, see in your son or daughter.

- "I'm sorry for . . ."

In this part of the letter, you try to make right the specific shortcomings and mistakes of the past. This is not the time to try to deal with your child's shortcomings.

- "I wish we could . . ."

This allows you to describe how you would like your relationship to be from now on.

A letter such as this may be one of the most important a mother or father will ever write. It is a beginning, but only a beginning. The letter must be followed by actions that consistently back up the words, and by conversations that attempt to build greater understanding on the foundation provided by the letter.

Upon receiving these thoughts in writing, will a son or daughter come running to a parent with a hug and a "happily ever after"? Probably not. The letter may initially be greeted with silence or, in a few cases, even hostility. But make no mistake about it—a letter like this, written positively and honestly, will go right to a child's heart. Whether or not the effect is visible or immediate, a parent has gone the extra mile to connect to a child's life.

FARMING A FAMILY

Space. That's what kids require in order to grow. Not the *Star Trek* kind or a bigger room (they can't even clean what they've got!). Emotional space and room to choose. Seldom will children change if it means admitting they were wrong or appearing to lose to Mom or Dad. They are most likely to change when they can have the dignity of choosing to change on their own.

That's what Laurie needed. Her mother was a single parent, frightened by Laurie's choice for a boyfriend. She was dating a thirty-five-year-old divorced man who had convinced this fourteen-year-old girl that this relationship was true love. Although Mom tried to restrict Laurie, she still found ways to be with her much older man. There was no convincing this teenage girl of the dangers, so her mother talked louder, longer, and more often about it. The nagging only drove her closer to the man and made her more defiant. Laurie's mother called me in as her last resort. I listened and then spelled out to Laurie the best reasons I could for bailing out of this dead-end relationship. No response.

I advised Mom to keep the restrictions she had established but not to bring up the subject again. "This has become a power struggle," I told her. "Laurie doesn't want to be humiliated by admitting she's made a mistake. Take the risk of giving her a little space for a while so she can have the dignity of making it her choice." As distraught as she was, Mom took my advice and kept silent.

Strangely enough, Laurie made an announcement to her mother about a month later. "I broke up with him," she said. "I got to thinking about the age difference, and I decided . . ." and she proceeded to list her reasons. They sounded strangely familiar to her mother and me. Laurie chose what was right when she was given room to choose.

So the fourth step in a strategy for a new beginning is to *allow some space*. If you don't, the new beginning may go aground on the rocks of discouragement. Better parents do not instantly get better sons and daughters. And the time lag between changes in a parent and response from a child can cause a mom or dad to despair that "it isn't working." Unless that parent understands the importance of space.

In some ways, parenting is farming, at least in an emotional and spiritual sense. A farmer has to be good at waiting. He knows you cannot sow corn seed on Monday and expect ripe corn on Tuesday. There's a period of time when it looks as if nothing is happening. If the farmer went out and dug around because "it isn't working," there might never be a crop. He plants, fertilizes, and walks away—for months. If, in his impatience, the grower kept pouring on water and fertilizer, he could kill the very crop he is trying to grow.

Now the closest you may have ever gotten to a farm may be the vegetable aisle at the grocery store, but if you are a parent, you are a farmer. When you present truth to a child on any issue, you are sowing seed in the decision-making part of that child. When you praise, hug, support, discipline, or train a son or daughter, you are sowing emotional seed to meet the needs they must have met at home. But, as every farmer can testify, there is a time lag between sowing and reaping.

A child-farmer (commonly known as a parent) tends to get impatient when the "crop" does not respond immediately. The seed may very well be growing invisibly under the surface, but it requires time and space. Most parents get frustrated because of the apparent lack of response and revert to that ancient family weapon called nagging. Unfortunately, too much nagging actually delays, and sometimes destroys, the harvest.

The older children get, the more they want the dignity of choosing. Over the years, I have discovered from many kids that they see the wisdom of their parents' advice far more frequently than they show. Many would choose that wisdom for themselves, if they were given the space to choose. But with Mom and Dad in hot and constant pursuit, it becomes a win/lose issue that a young man or woman does not intend to lose.

As Karen and I have farmed our "field," we have settled on a life-changing equation. It spells out the steps that are most likely to lead to a healthy human crop:

Truth + Space + Prayer & Unconditional Love = A Changed Life

Give a child the truth, then give him some un-nagged time to choose it. And what does a worried parent do during the long wait for results? Keep on loving, no matter what. And talk to God about it instead of constantly talking to your son or daughter about it. Your truth, your love, and God's power are a powerful combination for changing a young life.

When Lisa was in junior high, she used some of her money to make her first independent record purchase. As might be expected, she bought one we would not have bought. Actually, Lisa had made a basically good choice compared to the trashy choices available. She showed us the album, and all but two of the songs were totally innocent. Those two were not blatantly immoral, but they were questionable.

My first thought was to say, "No way, Lisa." But I knew she had to have practice in making her own decisions. So Karen and I briefly pointed out our concerns about the lyrics in question, and let her head upstairs to play her new prize. We gave her the truth, and nothing happened for two weeks, except her listening to that album. It was hard not to pursue the subject with Lisa, but we chose to pursue it with God instead.

Two weeks later, I was getting ready to take out the garbage (it was that time of year again), and suddenly I spied some unusually interesting trash. There in the garbage bag, broken in half, was that record. I breathed a sigh of relief and a prayer of thanks. Lisa had used the space to make a good choice, but it was *her* choice.

As a parent commits to a new beginning, he or she is saying, "I am going to set a course to meet the five heart-needs of this child instead of reacting to this child's deeds. And I will not base my actions on my child's immediate response." Needs-based parenting is a long-distance marathon, not a sprint.

WHO'S THAT CARRYING YOUR CHILD?

In the old TV show "Mission Impossible," it took a highly skilled team to get the job done. Jim Phelps, the leader of the pack, always began the show by sifting through photos of potential specialists he might choose for this seemingly undoable task—actors, electronics geniuses, special effects people, body builders, etc.

No such cast of specialists is needed for the raising of whole and healthy children at your house. Contrary to what our fears and inadequacies may tell us some days, parenting is not Mission Impossible. It is Mission Possible! It's not necessarily Mission Easy, but it is very doable. In fact, if a parent decides to have one good day at a time, being a parent can usually be Mission Enjoyable!

Understanding that your parent-mission is to meet those five heart-needs (a secure self; sexual answers; satisfying love; and two we are about to explore) provides hope and direction. Then you put to work the strategy for a new beginning:

- Put your past mistakes behind you.
- Have a good day.
- Write a letter.
- Allow some space.

Unfortunately, a parent's new beginning does not always guarantee happy endings. Kids are not scientific elements, responding automatically to a formula. There are no formula kids. Meeting their needs and pursuing this strategy provide the best possible environment for strong children to grow in. But no matter how conscientious and sacrificing a parent is, there will always be gaps.

As a parent, you will not be able to be all your children need. Life is too demanding, children are too complex, and parents are too limited. So the strategy for a new beginning requires one more vital step: *Trust God for the gaps.*

Several years ago, Karen and I rode bicycles across the romantic island of Nantucket. The island is "another world," about thirty miles off the coast of Cape Cod in Massachusetts. It was settled by the same kind of Puritan stock that landed at Plymouth Rock. Apparently, they understood something very powerful about raising a family.

We discovered that the early settlers' houses had door hinges that formed the letters "H" and "L." It was more than artwork. The letters stood for a prayer that still should adorn a home today, "Help, Lord."

If seventeenth-century parents needed "help, Lord," how much more must we twentieth-century parents need him. Especially when it comes to the gaps in our parenting. Whether a couple or a single parent, we just are not enough.

That's where a mom or dad must often say, "I can't, God. He's yours. She's yours." The One who gave us that child in the first place is the One we can most trust to carry them when we can't.

In fact, God makes an exciting promise to parents and children, and it's worth hanging on a wall somewhere.

> He [God] tends his flock like a shepherd. He gathers the lambs in his arms and carries them close to his heart. He gently leads those that have young. (Isaiah 40:11)

You probably carry a picture of those "lambs" in your wallet or purse. You know their names.

Many a night, when one of our children was far beyond our presence or influence, Karen and I have rested on this promise. "He gathers Lisa . . . He gathers Doug . . . He gathers Brad in his arms and carries them close to His heart." If you are a parent, you have a name of your own, your own lamb, to trust to His care. If you have done your best, the Great Shepherd will do the rest.

Many a time, when Karen and I have been baffled on what to do next as parents, we have put our names in the Shepherd promise. "He gently leads Ron and Karen, who have young." Again, your name in his promise may make all the difference for you. Yes—help, Lord.

From the moment of conception, having a child is a partnership with heaven. In one great act of human love, the potential for a child is created. But life cannot come from that love unless God does a life-giving miracle.

Parenting was a partnership when your child began, and it still is today. Your child cannot live without the love of Mom and Dad. But a parent's love is not enough.

A child's life continues to need the miracle touch of God.

Need

4

[#]

Stable
Authority

9

Authority
That Cripples a Child

Possum Trot is a real place. So are Deer and Blue Eye. And my wife wanted me to experience them. They are on some of the back roads of the Ozark Mountains in Arkansas.

For Karen, this is not tourist stuff; it is a sentimental journey back to the sights and memories of her childhood. For me, it is a journey back to "I have no idea where I am."

Karen had wanted to explore these beautiful mountain memories with me for years. Finally, we took a few days to do it. Our pilgrimage took the form of leaving the main road and venturing down peaceful, wooded byways that could have all been named "Rut Road." I enjoyed our second expedition more than I did our first.

That first exploration began at a dusty turnoff simply marked "Erbie." For all I knew, that was the name of a fellow who lived back there. It was actually a town we never saw.

Oh, we tried. We drove and drove, bouncing along the un-highway, stirring up dust, seeing nobody. I had left the main road with the confidence that my Arkansas honey knew where we were going. As it turned out, she didn't know and she didn't care.

Actually, I didn't care much either—the scenery and the greenery made me feel peaceful all over. Until, somewhere deep in the middle of nowhere, I looked at my gas gauge. It was flirting with the big "E." That's "E" for "empty." I was sure I had filled up with gas the day before, and I had not looked at my gauge all day.

All of a sudden, this expedition wasn't fun. I was light years from anything vaguely resembling civilization or a gas station. We did finally see one lady chopping her way through the underbrush to her pickup truck. I whimpered something about a gas station and she mumbled something about "left at the fork in the road."

The next minutes were hours. The wrong fork, backtracking uphill (that takes more fuel), and images of a long, cold night in the woods. I couldn't enjoy the scenery anymore, and my peace had turned to a cold sweat.

Well, we made it, but only on fumes. When I filled up, I'm sure I heard my gas tank whisper, "Oh, thank you!" The next day we did more back roads and this time in search of Possum Trot. But I completely enjoyed that trip. Believe me, my gauge was on "F" this time, and that's "F" for "full."

My country road close call was a vivid reminder that you should never head into unknown territory without a full tank!

Neither should our children. Every day is unknown territory for them, especially in a world where all the old moral maps are obsolete. Too many kids are getting lost, some of them never coming back. Others are not sure where the main road is or how to get through their day's journey. In order for a child to have an emotional tank full in a confusing world, a parent must provide clear, consistent directions. This underscores the critical importance of meeting the fourth need of our child. If parents fail to meet this need, the deficit will haunt a child for life.

It is clearly Mom and Dad who must *meet a child's need for stable authority*.

THE TEACHER, THE BOSS, AND BEYOND

Maybe it starts the first time a baby hears the word "no." But a child's first, and then most frequent, experiences with authority are at home. In fact, home is where most people decide how they will feel about all authority for the rest of their lives.

You probably did. Your parents, maybe one more than the other, shaped your concept of authority. If they were fair and consistent, you have probably done all right with people who are over you. If your parents were hypocritical or unyielding, you may be cynical or rebellious toward anyone telling you what to do. Permissive or neglectful parents may have left you with a malfunctioning conscience or confusion as to where the boundaries are. Abusive parents could have bequeathed to you anger and distrust. A perfectionist parent may have given you alternating spurts of drivenness and defeatedness.

Through their lives, your children will tend to act out the relationship to authority they learned from you. And that, of course, will affect their success and acceptance. If a child struggles with Mom or Dad's authority, he or she will probably struggle with the teacher, the boss, the rules, the boundaries, and even the Lord.

Their authority feelings will also affect their character. Character is rooted in internal controls which steer you to right and responsible choices, especially when no one is around. Those internal controls are learned from the external controls applied by your mother and father in your growing years. If parents exercise inadequate, inconsistent, or impossible authority, children often end up out of control inside. Living without the moral radar of character, they can easily crash.

If you are a parent, your child feels something about authority, and those feelings largely come from how you model, or don't model, authority in his or her life. Parents have a major responsibility to meet a child's decisive need for *stable authority*.

Someone might read that and respond, "Well, we're halfway there—our house looks like a stable." No, not that kind of stable. Children are looking for the kind of stable that means authority they can trust, respect, and depend upon.

Every parent is transmitting some kind of authority. Some styles of authority cripple a life, and other kinds build a life. Most of us never think about what our "command" is doing to our children. Most of us need to.

SEVEN CRIPPLING STYLES OF AUTHORITY

Divided authority damages kids. When Mom and Dad continually send conflicting signals, children find authority confusing. It is not uncommon for one parent to be the rock and the other the softie, one to be the drill sergeant and the other the therapist, or one to be the prosecutor and the other the defense. And that is not all bad if two perspectives merge and find a healthy balance.

What is unhealthy is when children learn they can play Mom and Dad against each other, and when "authority" leaves the ground rules unclear because it speaks with two voices. For parental authority to be respected, it must have one voice. Different drumbeats breed a rebel, first confused, ultimately cynical.

It is okay for parents to disagree on rules or discipline, just not in front of the kids! The bad seed planted in children by parental disagreement is just not worth it. If Mom and Dad want to do "fifteen rounds" verbally over how to handle the situation, let them do it a long way from the kids! Let them find one approach they can both stand for outside the "summit meeting." *It is more important for parents to be united on an issue than to be right.* Even if one parent has to "lose" to the other, it is far less expensive than a child losing respect for parental authority.

Four of the most powerful words in the parent arsenal are "Your father and I" or "Your mother and I." Case closed. Authority intact.

A second crippling approach is authority that is hypocritical. Mary told me that loud and clear when I talked to her about her self-destructive drug use. She was a teenager in a club program I ran, and she did not seem to care what she was doing to herself. When I asked what her parents had said to her about drugs, she sneered, "They told me not to." She paused and then ventured, "With the way my mother goes for the scotch every time she's got a problem, who is she to be telling me no?" A mother who escaped into alcohol had lost her right to tell her daughter not to escape into drugs.

The gap between words and actions may not be with a bottle. It can be a double standard about telling the truth, showing respect, admitting you're wrong, or being unselfish. A child may wonder what happened to the sweet, smiling saint at church when that saint turns into a sinner at home with hypocrisy that religious words cannot drown out. It is hard to believe a parent's verbiage about sexual purity when that parent's viewing choices portray just the opposite.

Kids may not often blow a whistle when they see chronic inconsistency, but they log it in their heart as a black mark against authority. Their "real-ometers" are finely tuned. Hypocrisy, like two-voiced authority, first confuses, then hardens a young person.

So the stable authority parent will understand the importance of honestly asking oneself, "Through my child's eyes, where am I saying one thing and living another?" and "How can I fix it?"

A third governing style that cripples a child is absentee authority. I have seen the weakness of that approach even when it does not involve children. A friend of mine owns a small rental house in the country, but he lives several hours away. He does what he can to keep the renters maintaining the property as they should. In reality, though, he seldom can be there to check on things and shape up the tenants. When the owner does drop in, he does not get many pleasant surprises, but frequently some unpleasant ones. The renters probably think, "He can tell us what to do all he wants. The fact is, he's not here." It is hard to exercise effective authority from a distance.

Unfortunately, too many parents try to do that. They are not home much, but they try to govern on the run. The "absentee landlord" parent barks out orders, is not there to follow through, and either never disciplines or disciplines ruthlessly. This is authority without contact, without understanding, without relationship. And authority that is not rooted in relationship usually produces a child who just sneers at authority or shuts down inside.

When mothers or fathers are disconnected from their kids, they do not even know who this child is becoming. The parents may flex their "I'm in charge" biceps and try to show they are in charge. But they will be responding to a stranger and disciplining a stranger. In order to govern a child properly, you have to know a child. In order to know a child, you have to be with him or her. That's why absentee authority is not stable authority—the parent, like my friend the landlord, is just too far away to really make a difference.

THE VOLCANO AND THE FUHRER

On my first visit to Ecuador, I was awed by the volcanoes that ring the capital of Quito and rule much of the countryside. As I stood with my mouth hanging open, my host pointed out the mountains I was admiring from his porch. The highest was Anasana, about 18,000 feet high. That dwarfed the tallest peaks I had ever seen in the majestic Rocky Mountains in America.

"Some experts believe Anasana used to be even higher," my host added, causing my mouth to gape open even more. He told me that some experts postulate that the peak was 28,000 feet high until it blew its top one day. Though the eruption only lasted a short time, the damage has lasted through the years.

Volcanic mothers and fathers have much the same effect on their children. They erupt, spew their "lava," blow away a piece of their child, and leave damage that lasts far longer than their eruption. This is uncontrollable authority, another kind that cripples a child's feelings about authority.

This kind of parent has given up any vestige of trying to be a thermostat in the home. Totally a thermometer, the volcanic mother or father is in a reactive mode, erupting upon provocation. While uncontrollable parents may evoke fear, they forfeit respect, and with it, possibly a child's respect for any authority. Children's ever-running recorders simply log the following data: "Authority is irrational, unfair, and out of control." It is not surprising that God pays high tribute to a person who is under control: "Better a patient man than a warrior, a man who controls his temper than one who conquers a city" (Proverbs 16:32).

If volcanoes could think, maybe they would think twice about blowing their top. "Maybe I'll feel better for a little while," a mountain might reason, "but is it worth blowing away a part of myself?" Parents can think, and they need to think about what their adult "tantrums" are costing them—a part of themselves called "my son" or "my daughter."

In addition to the crippling style of the volcano parent is the authority we might call "the fuhrer," or dictatorial authority. The dictator confuses authority with being authoritarian. Favorite sentences include, "Because I said so, that's why!" and "Just because I'm your father (mother), that's why!" No reason other than "I'm bigger than you are" or "I've got the badge."

Actually, these sentiments often are echoes of what a parent grew up with in his or her own childhood. Strangely, parents remember how it hurt and how little respect they felt. Fear, but not respect. Yet they try to control and squash their own kids as it was done to them.

Counselors and researchers have seen over and over that the authoritarian parent is the most likely, of all parenting styles, to produce a rebel. Yes, the dictator will get immediate compliance, but the "subject" will trash everything that parent values at the first opportunity. Ironically, that's the very outcome the mother or father was trying to avoid.

Authoritarians leave deep wounds on the hearts of the children they crush, and they create seething rebels who count the days until they can find a way to punish back.

A FILL-UP, NOT A FIX

Children grow up with the critical need for stable authority unmet when Mom and Dad offer one of the styles that cripple— authority that is divided, hypocritical, absentee, uncontrollable, or dictatorial. Two other styles leave a hole in a child where respect for authority should go.

One is manipulative authority—the kind that plays mind games with a child to get its own way. The script can read something like this: "How can you do this to me after all I've done for you? If you don't, I'm just not going to talk to you. I'm really hurting, but I'll just do it myself." Et cetera. The idea is to use guilt, pain, pity, pouting, silence, or whatever works to manipulate a child to do a parent's will. Again, like other distorted ways of governing, this approach may work, but only for the short haul.

If getting your way is your goal as a parent, manipulation may do the trick. But if your goal is raising a son or daughter who respects you and will respond to authority, you need to abandon manipulation as "not worth it." Manipulation breeds a smoldering resentment as a child thinks, *I know what Dad is doing . . . I hate this . . . but he makes me feel so crummy if I don't.* Children with those perceptions are recording that authority is selfish and guilt-filled, and it makes you "feel crummy." Not exactly a formula for a happy future in the area of authority.

Manipulative parents are too busy working on their own needs to really meet their children's needs.

The other style that cripples is not nearly as subtle—pushy authority. This species of parent is most often identified in the "Teenage Encyclopedia of Parents" as a "nag." The strategy here seems to be that the more times I say it, the more likely my child is to do it. Not necessarily.

If there is someone with you where you are, you can do your own exciting scientific experiment. Just go over to that person and push on him or her real hard. Now please observe, did that person come toward you or move away from you? This experiment should demonstrate the following hypothesis: the harder you push on people, the more likely they are to go the other direction. If you want someone to come your way, pushing is not the winning way to do it.

That usually holds true for a parent constantly pushing a child emotionally or verbally. Children pushed tend to be children who go the other way. If you repeat yourself you will eventually encounter the law of diminishing returns. Kids become immune to something they hear all the time, and sometimes they disregard important wisdom because it was neutralized by repetition.

As a parent, you cannot meet your child's need for stable authority if he or she is turning you off. That is what a child tends to do with a parent who is always pushing. It is more effective to make your case, enforce the boundaries at the first infraction, and, if it's an area where the child can choose, leave that child space to choose.

As we review the authority styles that cripple our kids, most of us parents find ourselves somewhere on the list, at least some of the time. The question is not whether we are imperfect authority models—that is a given. It is whether we acknowledge where we are failing and are willing to change. It may even mean an apology for any past damage done. If you just become defensive and rationalize your inadequacies, there is no hope of a better future.

Yes, our kids are deciding how to feel about authority based on how they feel about ours. They are deciding whether they one day will run from our values or make them their own. Their future character and success are on the line, based on how they relate to boundaries and authority.

Few areas of parenting are more affected by the way we were parented than this one. As we were yelled at, so we yell. As we were manipulated, so we manipulate. Or control or push or act hypocritically. And we, of all people, know how damaging those styles are, how they breed resentment and rebellion—not respect. If our children do not experience something more life-building, they will scar another generation when they copy us.

We need to move away from the authority that cripples to the authority that builds lives. Its six life-building ingredients are within the reach of every parent.

I learned on the "day of the empty gas tank" that the warning should not be confused with the real need. The red light that is next to the "E" on our gas gauge was glaring at me brightly. Frankly, the light was annoying. But the light was only a warning of the real problem. I didn't need to disconnect the light—I needed to fill an empty tank!

If a child is having problems with obeying or trusting or making good decisions, maybe the warning light is on. But the issue may not be the behavior that annoys or baffles Mom and Dad. It is an emotional fuel tank that needs some stable authority.

If our children need that kind of fill-up, then parents need to know which way the station is.

10

Authority
That Builds a Life

There aren't many rodeos on the south side of Chicago. Since that is where I grew up, I went many years without ever seeing a rodeo.

Feeling I had been tragically deprived, my wife, Karen, finally got me to one. I enjoyed every minute of it! One reason was the emcee-on-horseback, whose colorful comments added to the energy of the event. He told who the competing cowboys were, what was significant about each competitor's time, and what to expect in the next event. He even read the cows' minds for us!

At the end of the calf-roping competition, there were two calves who had no intention of cooperating with the riders who were trying to clear the arena. Those white-faced critters were darting every direction to avoid being rounded up. Calves 2, Cowboys 0.

That was when the emcee drawled what he was sure those rebellious calves were thinking: "I don't wanna. I ain't gonna."

Those two sentences may summarize how the two-legged "calves" at your house feel about authority. Most of us have an instinctive resistance to the word *no*, to discipline, to boundaries. "We don't want to, and we ain't going to." Yet a child's ability to live within authority and within boundaries is fundamental to his or her character and success.

So parents, life's first and foremost authority influences, have the assignment of making "authority" a positive word in a child's heart. Authority has become a negative, angry, or meaningless concept for many because parents used one or more of the crippling varieties described in the last chapter.

Now it is important to focus on the kind of stable authority that builds a life instead of tearing it down. An effective parent will govern using the seven ingredients in life-building authority.

1. THE PREPARATION OF LISTENING

Listening may seem like a curious component of authority, but you have to find out where those "calves" are before you can round them up! The parents who are listened to by their children win the right to be heard by listening to their children.

Unfortunately, listeners are an endangered species in our over-stuffed lifestyles. You can prove this the next time you lose your train of thought in the middle of a sentence. You will probably look at the person you are talking to and ask in frustration, "What was I saying?" And that person will have no idea what you were saying. You will know that by his or her silent tongue, darting eyes, and vacant expression. In fact, you could probably count on one hand the number of times anyone has known what you were saying in your forgetful moment.

Listening is the fulcrum of healthy relationships and appropriate authority. When mothers or fathers do not take time to hear their children's questions, perspectives, and feelings, they are governing strangers and risking miscalculations. Lecture-without-listen parenting might be likened to a physician who prescribes a cure before the patient tells his or her symptoms. Imagine . . . you walk into the doctor's office, and before you can even say "hi," he decrees, "Penicillin!" "But, Doctor," you would probably protest, "you don't have any information about how I'm feeling." You would not be happy if he simply says, "Look, I am the doctor. You need penicillin." It is hard to trust authority that does not listen before it prescribes.

The Bible is straightforward in its evaluation of people who live by monologue, not dialogue: "He who answers before listening, that is his folly and his shame" (Proverbs 18:13). Then, in advice that should be on a conspicuous wall plaque in every home, the Bible says: "Everyone should be quick to listen, slow to speak and slow to become angry" (James 1:19).

No, not quick to speak and slow to listen, which is unfortunately the authority style of many moms and dads. "Me parent, you kid. Me speak, you listen." We parents tend to hear one sentence and assume we know the rest of the paragraph. We hear a few words and sometimes never hear their heart. And we offer a quick prescription without ever listening to the patient. Unlistening parents breed resenters, rather than respecters, of authority; exploders, rather than expressers; and shutting down, rather than sharing.

So an important starting point for a parent's life-building authority might be asking this question, "Would my son or daughter call me a good listener?" If the answer is yes, you have the credibility upon which effective authority is founded. When parents genuinely listen to their children, it prepares them to lead with understanding. And it prepares their child to be led because "my parents know where I'm coming from."

Listening to a child is more than the absence of talking. It is a very active process—a determination to understand what is underneath this attitude or action. Apparently, that is not what Megan thought her mother was doing one day in the laundry room. Megan had just come home from school and found her mom getting clothes out of the dryer and folding them. The teenager announced, "I've got something to tell you, Mom."

"Go ahead, honey, I'm listening" was Mom's response as she continued to fetch and fold.

Megan pressed her need a little, "I need you to listen, Mom."

Another reassurance that "I'm listening" followed as laundry kept moving. Finally, in frustration, Megan sputtered, "Well, your hands aren't!"

Actually, Megan had a point. Real listening is something all of you does, not just your ears. But we busy adults often seem afflicted by the curse of preoccupation, which tells our kids that at least part of us is somewhere else when they are talking to us. Unintentionally, we convey the feeling that we are either coming from or going to something more important than they are.

The listening in life-building authority is totally focused attention—eyes, ears, hands. It asks second and third questions to be sure there is understanding. It makes a child feel, if only for a brief time, as if he or she is the only person on this planet for that moment.

Realistically, that kind of attention is often not possible with phones, deadlines, responsibilities, and the rest of the family consuming you. If you can't really listen now, set a time when you can. "It's going to take me about an hour to finish this. Frankly, you're only going to get part of me if we talk right now. Give me an hour and then you've got all of me." Sometimes a listening window may even be in a day or two (no, not next month!), if a child can wait. Be sure you are there when promised. Other times your child won't wait, and your parent-radar may blink, "You'd better drop everything and listen now. Later may not happen." In general, a child's need for Mom or Dad's listening ear has a short shelf-life, and parents need to hear it at the earliest possible opportunity. Missing the moment does not mean what a child had to say was not that important; it probably means he or she just gave up.

Some parents complain, "I wish there was something to listen to—my kid doesn't talk!" One reason may be that Mom and Dad are failing the test of the little things. Children watch what happens when they try to tell their parents about the seemingly small stuff of their lives. If a parent seems bored or disinterested, a child may conclude that he or she will never share the big things. Actually, the little things of kids' lives are big things to them. If you flunk the test of the small matters, you will probably never hear the matters that really count.

Another reaction that can shut children down is when parents betray shock at what is shared. A parent can be melting down inside with shock, but the shock must never make it to the face or the mouth. Most kids are so afraid of disappointing their parents that they withdraw at the first sign of parental shock. The parent who remains cool when the information is hot is most likely to learn more.

Children may stop talking, too, if they feel their parents are telling other people what was confided in them, or if the information they shared is later used against them in a heated moment. If someone betrays our information or bludgeons us with it, we are likely to stop talking. Where that has been the case, a parent's apology and request for forgiveness may reopen communication.

There cannot be good authority-seed sown in a child without communication. Listening parents create a climate in which children will open up their lives. When children really feel heard, they respect the authority of the one who heard them. They won't always agree with the listening parent, but they will record on their "tapes" that authority is fair and "trustable."

In a sense, our children are holding up a big sign whenever they try to talk to us. The sign asks, "Is what I say important to you?"

A "no" will close their life. A "yes" will open it wide.

2. THE PREDICTABILITY OF DISCIPLINE

Out of bounds. Every athlete understands those words. In football, for example, there are all kinds of exciting things players can do—they can pass the ball, run the ball, kick the ball, tackle each other, block each other. But they have to do it in bounds.

From the moment football teams march out onto the field, they know where the boundaries are. Imagine the chaos if Bronco Gorillski, star running back, started running for a touchdown, saw he was about to be tackled, and decided to finish his run up in the stands. Bronco leaps over the bench, bowls over two cheerleaders on the sidelines, and charges up into the fourteenth row, where he continues his touchdown run. He can do that because this particular game is being played on a field with no boundaries! As Bronco knocks down one last hot dog vendor in his way, he finishes his ninety-five-yard run, while, down on the field, the referees are still trying to decide if he is out of bounds.

Obviously, you cannot have a game without clear boundaries. You cannot have a life without them either! Yet many a family has no clear boundaries, which are learned through consistent enforcement. Children invariably keep testing the limits, waiting for the whistle to blow. If the boundaries keep changing, and if the whistle sometimes blows early, sometimes late, and sometimes never, it's hard for a son or daughter to be sure what is really out of bounds. And that is unstable authority in a life that has a "must meet" need for stable authority.

In addition to clear boundaries, there must also be clear penalties. In football, every player knows in advance how many yards his team will be penalized if he grabs a face mask, roughs a kicker, or blocks illegally. In basketball, there is no question as to what kinds of moves will cost you a foul. Once there is a violation, there is no long discussion on the field or court about what the penalty should be, because that has been decided long before the first kickoff or tip-off.

Again, children need that same kind of structure to give their lives stability. Effective parents provide an unmistakable answer to a child's unspoken question about the rules, "What if I don't?" Clear boundaries, clear penalties.

Those two components make up the second ingredient in life-building authority—the predictability of discipline. In other words, children need to know exactly what they will be disciplined for, and what kind of discipline it will be. A mother or father who provides this sort of predictability is teaching one of life's most indispensable lessons: actions have consequences. Parents have few responsibilities greater than modeling for their children one of the "Laws of the Universe": the Law of Sowing and Reaping. Or, in the straightforward words of the Ultimate Parenting Book, "A man reaps what he sows" (Galatians 6:7). Children who do not consistently experience this law at home are destined to make a lifetime of destructive decisions and tragic miscalculations.

God's parenting instructions include some strong statements about discipline: "He who spares the rod hates his son. He who loves him is careful to discipline him" (Proverbs 13:24).

To discipline is to love. Failing to discipline is failing to love.

It is important for a parent to distinguish between discipline and punishment. Discipline is to teach; punishment is to unload anger. Discipline is reasoned; punishment is inflamed emotion. Discipline is thought through; punishment is too enraged to think. When parents discipline, they are working on their child's needs, but when they simply punish, parents are working mostly on their own needs.

I have seen that dynamic at work in some public parent/child showdowns. It's usually in a store where a child has disobeyed or embarrassed a parent. How does this mother or father respond to an out-of-control child? By becoming an out-of-control parent!

The parent grabs the child by one arm and begins to yank that arm every possible direction, while spewing out heated words through clenched teeth. The moment that began with the mother or father being embarrassed has now embarrassed all of us in the store! One gets the distinct feeling that there is no real teaching (discipline) going on at this moment, only venting (punishment).

The learning of boundaries and penalties is just too critical for a child to miss or a parent to mess up. Without a plan, Mom and Dad are likely to fail in meeting this need. Few areas of parenting are more confusing and challenging than this area of consistent discipline. The confusion comes from a babble of voices— talk show experts who don't agree; other parents' approaches to discipline ("You're no fair, Mom! Jimmy's parents let him!"); a plethora of conflicting books on the subject; the memories of how your parents did it.

In addition, no two families are the same, and certainly no two children are! The approach that is strong enough to shape one child may be so strong it sinks another child in the same family. Different kids require different proportions of firmness and flexibility, toughness and tenderness. That is why listening is such an important ingredient. It provides the understanding required to discipline each child in his or her language. But different kids can still play on the same family field with the same clear boundaries and clear penalties.

As every parent of multiple children has learned, kids are great scorekeepers. Especially when it comes to how their siblings are being "officiated." On a number of occasions, one of our three children has complained that "you didn't do anything" to a brother or sister. And on that same number of occasions, Karen and I have had to remind them that discipline is a private matter between a parent and a child. What you, as a parent, do with one child is no sibling's business! Each child needs to know that crossing a boundary will result in a private reckoning, behind closed doors. While there are many variables in disciplinary decisions, there is a plan that can be applied in every family. The plan includes four steps to consistent discipline.

First, there are boundaries and penalties decided in advance. Again, you do not start playing the game and then try to figure out where the lines are. Every player in the family must understand the boundaries and penalties up front!

So, moms and dads cannot make it up as they go along. They must take the time to settle the rules and ramifications before there is an incident. In a two-parent home, this may require some hard conversations and hard choices. But family peace is the product of clear and consistent rules.

The alternative is trying to make authority choices in the heat of a confrontation. Heat seldom produces choices you will be proud of; good decisions require light, not heat. Parents are not at their disciplinary best yelling by the front door at midnight or with a bad report card in their hands. "That's it! You're grounded for a year!" Irrational, even unenforceable, edicts are usually issued when discipline is decided on the spot. No, life-building boundaries and penalties are decided *in advance*.

Secondly, they are *discussed* in advance. The older kids get, the more they should have some input before boundaries and penalties are decided. A parent's "script" for a discussion of discipline might go something like this:

"We're working on how to handle _____ now that you're getting older and more mature. We've got some ideas on it, but we would like to hear what you think is a fair rule in this area. Also, what do you think should happen if you don't stay 'in bounds'? Tell us what you think, and we'll tell you our thoughts on it. After we've talked about it with you, we'll make some decisions, and we'll make sure you're the first to know what we decide!"

Children need to understand that they will not decide the boundary or penalty, but they will have input before the decision is made. Once the policy is set, it should be given to a son or daughter with the reasons for it, and at a quiet time when there is no blood-boiling incident in progress. Boundaries and penalties seem arbitrary and punitive when they come in the context of an explosive incident. They seem much more valid when they come from the light of a discussion rather than the heat of a showdown.

The third step in the plan for predictable discipline is boundaries and penalties that are consistently enforced. The busier a parent's life, the tougher this is to do. It seems inconvenient to stop for immediate discipline. Many parents often wait until a child's behavior has reached critical proportions. It is much easier to cool down the reactor at the first sign of trouble than to deal with a meltdown. If the ax sometimes falls sooner and sometimes later, and sometimes never (depending on how busy or tired Mom and Dad are), the rules become blurred and confusing.

In reality, taking time to enforce the rule early is ultimately saving time. For boundaries to stick, a parent has to pursue enforcement aggressively at first, until a child concludes that this is serious. Eventually, what Mom or Dad once had to police closely will usually become self-policed. Stay with it in the early stages, and blow the whistle as soon as their toes touch the boundary line.

Finally, the plan involves boundaries and penalties that are fair. That means that the penalty fits the crime. Usually, a proportionate disciplinary response requires some thought. And that requires a little time. Anger is not your friend in disciplining sensibly. In fact, the Bible warns that "man's anger does not bring about the righteous life that God desires" (James 1:20). In other words, you won't do anything right when you're angry!

Thoughtful discipline backs off briefly and asks, "What kind of discipline would be a logical consequence I could attach to this action?" If the problem is with a child's mouth, then maybe that mouth should not be used for a while. If the issue is with the car or the phone, the penalty should involve that area. I know one family who chose a creative response to children's things left scattered through the house. Mom and Dad had a "Saturday Box," where they locked up anything they found lying on the floor. When a child asked where his or her "whatever" was, the Saturday Box was the answer. The box was opened every Saturday for reclaiming purposes. The parents simply explained, "When I find something lying around and out of its place, it seems to me that it isn't important enough to you to take care of. So I just put it away in the Saturday Box." The point is that the discipline was fair because it fit the "crime."

Logical consequence discipline clearly demonstrates the Law of Sowing and Reaping. At the moment, "fair" might not be the word a child is thinking, because they were hoping to get away with it. Fair, solid discipline stands the test of time. It looks responsible a month later, a year later, a lifetime later.

If your children are being raised in a climate where discipline is predictable, they are learning stable authority. Your consistent "officiating" will give them the security that can only come from clear boundaries and clear penalties.

Then they can run all of life's exciting plays, and they will know the secret of playing without regrets—all the things that count are inside the boundaries.

3. THE PRIORITIZING OF BATTLEGROUNDS

At the Battle of Little Bighorn, General Custer did not get to choose his battleground. It was not a happy ending.

Many parents make a similar mistake—they do not choose their battlegrounds! The older children get, the more skirmishes there are, especially as their freedom increases and a parent's penalty options decrease. If Mom and Dad make every battle a major battle, they will run out of ammunition!

That is why it is important to decide which battles are worth fighting. By implication, parents are then deliberately deciding to hold their fire on other battles. "Does this one really matter?" is a mental check a parent may need to use several times a day.

The plan for consistent discipline must include this third step of prioritizing the battlegrounds. Otherwise, there is almost constant warfare in a home. Conflict should be the exception in a well-governed family, not the rule. Obviously, conflict will be a way of life if a parent tries to make everything about a child right.

Maybe it's perfectionism that cannot leave a flaw unconfronted, and that often creates children who either go wild or go off the deep end. Perhaps a parent has a perverse need to control. Or it's an insecure parent who has to keep winning and proving he or she is in charge. Some mothers and fathers suffer from a "messiah complex" that tells them they are the only ones who can fix this child.

Whatever the parent's needs, the child's need for stable authority goes unmet when authority is always nagging, pursuing, reacting, and fighting. A discerning parent knows that silence is sometimes as golden as speaking. When it is a nonbearing issue, a stable authority says, "I'll let this one pass."

A battle with a happier ending than Custer's was the Battle of Bunker Hill. In the early days of the American Revolution, the British repeatedly charged the ragtag American force, which was holding a strategic hill near Boston. The Americans continually repelled the larger, more professional British Army. One reason was the famous command given in the heat of battle: "Don't fire until you see the whites of their eyes!"

Hold your fire until it really counts. That's a winning strategy, especially when it comes to parents saving their ammunition for the battles that really matter.

4. PRACTICING FREEDOM

There are parents with feathers who have something to teach us. Mother Eagle, to be precise. My friends from eagle country tell me that she realizes her babies need a little help venturing out of the nest. So when the eaglets are getting old enough to learn to fly, Mother Eagle starts to "uncomfort" the nest. She starts to put sharp sticks and stones inside so Baby Eagle will be motivated to get out and soar. The result is majestic.

Mother Eagle's lesson? "If your kids are ever going to fly, you need to be an ally of their freedom." Unfortunately, many children get the impression that they have to fight their mother and father to get out of the nest!

The reality is that our children will be on their own someday, making virtually all their decisions without us. In most families, the weaning process starts early. There's the day you leave them at the kindergarten door; the day they start grade school, middle school, high school; their first sleepover; their first drive; their first date (any time after they turn twenty-six, of course). And in between the milestones, there are hundreds of little decisions our children make without us parents around.

As a parent, you are pretty sure you can make responsible decisions for your child. But can your child make responsible decisions for himself or herself? *Not without practice!* That is why one key ingredient in life-building authority is providing practices with freedom.

Our own kids are old enough now to begin to analyze what their parents did with them, and to them. Recently, we had a "roll on the floor" time of laughing as they told us how our discipline felt from their side. Why couldn't they have told us at the time?

Lisa and Doug were together recently, and somehow Mom and Dad came up in the conversation. We were eight hundred miles away, totally unaware we were under the microscope. I'm sure they discussed our weaknesses, and they were kind enough not to tell us about that part. But Lisa and Doug did tell us some things they agreed we had done right.

One of them was what they called "gradual freedom." Our kids said, "You let us test our wings as we went along, while we were still at home. You didn't wait 'til college to let us try some freedom . . . and then go crazy!"

What our kids do not know is the great uncertainty we had in making many of those freedom choices. There was no specific blueprint to follow, and we were seldom sure what was too much or too little latitude. But we had a guiding principle that freedom should not be sudden; it must be learned gradually and progressively.

Freedom practice involves a precious, precarious bond called *trust*. Freedom practice requires parental trust. The parents' secret is this: as they spend more and more time away from us, what choice do we have but to trust them? Of course, we do not want our children to know we have figured this out. Instead, we want to make their inevitable freedom a bond between us rather than a barrier.

Preparing children for independence essentially boils down to this: *parents who offer trust and children who earn it*. It sounds something like this:

"We know you're going to be on your own more and more now, and one day you'll be making all your own decisions. That's why we want you to be able to experiment with more and more freedom while you're still with us. But freedom can be a dangerous thing if you're not ready for it. We just need to know that you're ready for the growing freedom we want to give you. If you show us you can be trusted with the freedom and responsibility we've already given you, we'll give you more and more."

In this way, a mother or father is offering a pathway to freedom. The first milestone on that path is regular responsibility. Kids need specific, regular "chores" and areas for which they are responsible. These are proving grounds that demonstrate how a child handles things. The reward is greater freedom—with the phone, the weekend, the friends, the homework, etc.

The second milestone on the pathway to freedom is experimental privileges. For example, if you prove you can handle a 10:30 curfew, you've got 11:00, then 11:30, etc. (within reason!). If you get good grades, you can have more say in when you do your homework. If you keep your grades up, you can be in that sport. If you drive responsibly in our town, you have won the right to drive outside our town. This approach is based upon a principle laid down by the only perfect Father, "Whoever can be trusted with very little can also be trusted with much" (Luke 16:10).

The third milestone on the pathway to freedom is informing headquarters. Children earn trust by calling often to keep Mom and Dad informed of their whereabouts. In our family, we called this the "No Surprises" policy. Call when your plans change; call when you're going to be late; call when you've gotten in trouble, because we want to hear it from you; call to tell us you won't be home for dinner—just keep in touch with headquarters!

Even when they are little, children should be given little freedom practices—privileges that grow as they show they can be trusted. This trustworthiness freedom cycle is parenting at its best—practically preparing your child to live without you.

Sometimes a son or daughter will fail a freedom test. A parent generally needs to allow the reaping to come, without intervening. It is far better for them to have their first struggles and stumbles with freedom while they are still with Mom and Dad, while there is someone there to hug them, debrief them, correct them, even pray with them.

Trust offered, trust earned. That is the kind of authority style that builds a child who makes "no regrets" choices.

Mother Eagle has the right idea. Do not perch on the edge of the nest, trying to keep your "eaglets" in as long as possible.

Encourage them to get out of the nest and to try some short flights. They probably won't be too graceful at first, they may fly too far sometimes, and they may need you to break their fall—but let them fly! One day they will soar on their own, and even build a nest of their own. All because you helped them know how to live outside the nest.

5. THE PERSPECTIVE OF HUMOR

"A cheerful heart is good medicine" (Proverbs 17:22). That Bible-recommended medication could help heal many a family malady!

It may seem odd to recommend the perspective of humor as one of the ingredients in life-building authority. But, in fact, many parents would have more authority if they would lighten up a little! The more a family has stress and struggles, the more a mom or dad tends to take life very seriously, and sometimes too seriously. The problems and tensions tend to become each day's centerpiece, and the consumed parent begins to lose perspective. In addition, "uptightness" makes the rest of the family want to get away from Mr. or Mrs. Intense. He or she is wearing them out!

That is where a sense of humor helps, and the ability to stand back from a situation and laugh at it, or even at yourself. The parent who can kid about his or her own weaknesses goes up on a child's respect scale. By diffusing the tension around an irritated issue, a person helps everyone involved see more clearly.

If you are a parent, it might be worth a moment just to ask yourself, "Am I taking things too seriously, including myself?" And if you are really daring, ask your mate or your children. Should there be a "yes" vote, try the Doctor's prescription for healthier relationships: "a cheerful heart." Lighten up a little!

6. THE PULL OF VULNERABILITY

They may be the three hardest words of all to say . . ."I was wrong." The parent who never says them will pay a high price in respect.

Anyone who was raised by a "never wrong" mother or father can attest to that. A proud rigidity did not make that parent seem taller, only smaller. An unwillingness to admit mistakes or apologize breeds resentment in a child, not respect. Yet, tragically, the wounded sons and daughters of invulnerable parents tend to become "never wrong" parents themselves.

There seems to be a perverse little voice inside that whispers, "If you're going to have their respect, you cannot ever show you're weak." In reality, healthy human beings do not care who is right, they care about what is right. For me, that has meant late-night trips to the bed of a five-year-old son to say, "I'm sorry for the way I talked to Mom and you tonight. I was wrong. Will you forgive me?" That is hard, but it's the only honest thing to do. Wrong is wrong, and I need to be able to admit it. Right is right, even if it means a little boy is right and his big daddy is wrong.

The pull of vulnerability contributes strongly to life-building authority. The ability to be wrong makes authority approachable, reasonable, and genuine, not hypocritical. "Never wrong" hardens people and problems; "I was wrong" heals them. Or, in the words of the Bible: "Confess your sins to each other and pray for each other so that you may be healed" (James 5:16).

How many marriages could have been saved if someone could have been wrong? How many kids could have been saved if a parent could have said, "I was wrong"? It is never too late to say those words to your children, even if they have children of their own. That admission is where healing begins—at any age.

No, being a vulnerable parent will not cost you your child's respect—it will earn it!

7. THE POWER OF DIGNITY

Our son Doug has never been hard to find at home. He has been kind enough to leave a trail of clothes, shoes, and Doug-stuff wherever he goes. Follow the trail, and you'll find him.

While Doug has not been noted for his neatness, there is one area of his life that defies the usual pattern—his baseball cards. What began as a little kid's hobby has become a young man's personal assets. Doug has invested very wisely in baseball cards that will appreciate exponentially. Yes, it is a kingdom of cardboard, but it is worth a lot!

Doug knows the value of those cards, so he takes very good care of them. Unlike any of his other possessions, the cards are organized, cataloged, protected. When you ask him why they get such unusual attention, Doug replies, "Dad, these things lose value if they get a crease or a stain or a rounded corner. They're too valuable to let them get messed up."

If that is true of some pricey cardboard, it is surely true of children handmade by God. That is the bottom-line appeal of a parent to a child, "You are too valuable to get messed up." Listening to a son or daughter says, "You are important." Trusting a son or daughter says, "You are competent." Disciplining a son or daughter says, "You are worth so much that I will fight anything that might hurt you."

When children are hearing the siren song of cheapening choices, they need parents who are saying, "Not you—you're too valuable for that." When they are looking down a dead-end street just because so many of their peers are on it, they need an authority person who says, "Not you—remember what you're worth." When they are willing to settle for mediocrity, they must have a mom or dad reminding them, "Not you—you can be so much more."

Ultimately, stable authority is rooted in the power of dignity. It gives children dignity by treating them with respect. It preserves children's dignity by keeping them in bounds and teaching them how to choose. It appeals, then, to a child's dignity to steer them away from the edge of the cliff.

Crippling authority crucifies a child, but life-building authority dignifies a child. Because our children are all like those rodeo calves, "I don't wanna and I ain't gonna," even the best parental authority will encounter anger, resistance, and many anxious moments. Moms and dads will always wonder if they are doing the right thing in situations that have no formula. Being in charge of a developing life will always be a challenge.

But remember, underneath their deeds is a fundamental, life-shaping need—the need for stable authority. After all is said and done, that need is ultimately met by two gold-medal words—*consistency* and *respect*.

Consistency is communicated by a parent whose words and life match, who provides predictable structure, and who stays on his or her moral course, even while other parents vacillate in confusion.

Respect is communicated when parents listen to their children with all their heart, explain the "whys" behind the "musts," and prepare them to win with discipline and trust. Stable authority, while often not appreciated at the moment, ultimately makes a child feel very, very important, and ready to live a life that is under control in an out-of-control world.

BAD NEWS, GOOD NEWS

The journey to understanding our child's needs is nearing its end. We have traveled behind their behavior to see what their hearts are really crying for—a secure self, sexual answers, satisfying love, and stable authority.

Now, on the threshold of the fifth and greatest need of all, we come face-to-face with bad news. While the agenda for parenting may be clearer than ever to us, so are our limitations and our own needs.

Frankly, to be this kind of parent is humanly impossible. Our hearts may want it, but our resources cannot fully deliver on all these needs.

Which leads us to the Good News . . .

Need

#5 Spiritual Reality

11

No Unguided Missiles

The day we brought that wiggling yellow blanket into our little apartment couldn't have been very long ago. The baby girl inside had changed everybody's name in the family. Karen's sister was now Aunt Val, our parents were suddenly Grandma and Grandpa, and, most overwhelming of all, my wife was now Mommy and I would be, from that day on, Daddy.

Baby Lisa and I spent a lot of hours together in those nights when I took the 2:00 A.M. feeding. That was when I had hair and she didn't. Today she has lots of hair, and I—well, a lot has changed. Wasn't it just yesterday that I cradled her in my arms, looked into those big blue eyes, and talked to her about things she wouldn't understand for twenty years?

Nowadays, as I speak with Lisa and her husband on the phone, it is obvious that the years have raced by on "fast forward." Maybe that is why I jokingly requested that one song not be played at her wedding, "Sunrise, Sunset." It is hard to walk your daughter down the aisle without asking yourself, "Is this the little girl I carried?" Our sons are not married, but I am already asking, "Is this the little boy at play?"

I was only allowed in the delivery room for the birth of one of our three children. We were ready for me to be there before the medical community was. By the time our youngest, Brad, was born, the hospitals finally thought dads might like to be there for the arrival. Today they have every option in the delivery room but a film crew and a marching band. Like I said, a lot has changed.

I will never forget that magic moment when Brad had just made his entrance and Dr. Eisner asked, "Would you like to hold him?" Brad was two minutes old the first time I held him, and one word flooded my heart as I did — "miracle." Suddenly, I heard the doctor speaking what I was thinking, "This is the greatest miracle known to man."

It wasn't ultimately that physician who placed this life in my hands—it was God. Three times—Lisa, Doug, then Brad—the Creator had trusted an unmarked life into my trembling hands. Karen and I would have eighteen years to mark this person, for better or for worse. We would be shaping this child, whether we realized it or not. This child was unformed clay in our hands. God was saying, as He says to every mom or dad, "Here is My creation, entrusted to you. Mark this child well."

In the delivery room or at the 2:00 A.M. feeding, it seems as if you have a long time to shape the clay. At their graduation or wedding, you wonder where the time went. And one day, sooner or later, you realize you had nothing more important to do than to shape that young life.

We can't have any wasted days back. But today is the first day of the rest of your life with that son or daughter. Your child carries needs that the Creator assigns you to meet. And whether you have many or few "sunrise, sunsets" left in that child's life, those needs can be your focus. Then the rest of your days together can be the best of your days together.

Unfortunately, it is easy to forget our mission. Our children's deeds are so loud we cannot hear their needs. So we parents tend to spend ourselves mostly on the deeds we can see rather than the needs we cannot see, reacting to what they are doing instead of acting on why they are doing it. That is why our journey in this book has pursued the five heart-needs God intended for our children to have met at home. By addressing the need that fuels the deed, we are stepping up to proactive parenting and building people who are strong from the inside out. They know they are "fine china," too valuable to throw away, because Mom and Dad have given them the gift of a Secure Self. They will keep sex inside the fence of love and commitment because of the Sexual Answers with which their parents have fortified them. They will not look for love in all the wrong places because they have gotten it from the right place, Satisfying Love from parents who loved them in their language. They will not live "out of control" because they have tasted Stable Authority in the loving leadership at home.

Yet, with those needs being met, a child is still incomplete. In fact, if each need could be thought of as a hole in a child's heart, this last hole would be the biggest one of all. If it is empty, then a parent has missed the mission that matters most. There is one more heart-need that should be met at home: *your child's need for spiritual reality.*

Ironically, this need brings you back to the moment when your baby changed your name to Mommy or Daddy, when that unmarked life was placed in your hands. And it brings you to the One who trusted you with his creation.

DANGEROUS MISSILES

I have never been close to an Intercontinental Ballistic Missile (ICBM) before. I have never wanted to be. But recently, I was very close to many ICBMs.

I had been invited to speak for a week on an Air Force base. This base happened to be the home of a number of missiles with nuclear warheads. It is certainly not a national secret that they are housed in underground silos, often right in the middle of a farm. The cows who graze nearby are rumored to glow in the dark.

Actually, this missile defense system is very impressive. Of course, I was not given any classified information, but I was privileged to see some of America's powerful defense from up close. Inside each of those silos is a missile that will go up to 6,000 miles, punched into the sky by a fiery launch beneath the ground. And it knows where it's going!

That is a good thing. The ICBM's internal guidance system is what directs it to its target and keeps it from deadly detours. The power of a missile is frightening enough, but imagine if all that power were unleashed without a guidance system!

That is also a frightening prospect when it comes to children. They are powerful "missiles." High-powered education has wired them with informed minds. They are socially aware, sexually aware, and physically developed earlier than ever. But for many, there is something alarmingly missing—an internal guidance system. They have well-developed minds and well-developed bodies, but often, underdeveloped souls. Without a strong spiritual guidance system inside, a child can "have it all" and still go astray or self-destruct.

A parent may raise a child who is physically attractive, mentally sharp, and socially skilled, and still leave him or her spiritually unprovided for. To paraphrase a famous question asked by Jesus Christ, "What shall it profit a parent if your child gains the whole world, and loses his own soul?"

Some parents might respond, "We have provided everything our child needed, including a religion." These parents have recognized that there is a spiritual dimension their child needs and have done something to meet it. While religion is a step in the right direction, it is unfortunately not enough. Kids need spiritual reality, and religion alone cannot be that for them.

When the nuclear submarine Thresher vanished in the Atlantic years ago, the experts tried to determine a cause. It turned out that the Thresher had gone deeper than she was pressurized to dive, and the hull collapsed. The crew was lost, all because the pressure on the outside became greater than the pressure on the inside.

That is a reason so many kids are collapsing today. They feel crushed by peer pressure, parent pressure, academic pressure, sexual pressure, family pressure. Unless the pressure on the inside of a child is greater than the pressure on the outside, collapse is inevitable. Spiritual reality is God-strength on the inside, powerful and personal enough to hold together, no matter what the pressure.

If parents do not meet their child's need for spiritual reality, they are launching an unguided missile in a world filled with tempting, destructive detours. They are sending a son or daughter into deep water without the inner strength to withstand the relentless pressure.

Of all the needs we parents are responsible to meet, this one can uncover the greatest feeling of inadequacy. Worth and love and discipline are one thing, but how does a parent develop a child who is spiritually ready? Thankfully, the One who asks us to do it also tells us how.

PASSING ON A PERSON

A supermarket of sexual possibilities. A violent culture. A generation who has not worked for anything and has been given everything. Parents facing questions from their kids that no previous parents have had to answer.

Sound familiar? Sound like the challenges we parents are facing today? Like the last days of the twentieth century? According to the Bible, it also described the fifteenth century before Christ!

The Ultimate Parenting Book portrays a parenting challenge very much like ours, only against an ancient backdrop. Ancient, but strangely familiar. The ancient Jews were just moving into the land we call Israel and they called Canaan. They had been together with like-minded, like-faith people for an entire generation of wilderness wandering. Suddenly they were in Canaan, a culture steeped in sexual depravity and violence. Now how could a parent raise spiritually healthy kids in that kind of infected environment? When God told them how, He was also telling us.

Here is God's Parenting Plan for a moral minefield: "Love the Lord your God with all your heart and with all your soul and with all your strength. These commandments I give you today are to be upon your hearts. Impress them on your children."

Actually, the spiritual reality a child needs begins in the heart of the parents. It's like those oxygen masks they demonstrate on every airplane flight I take. The flight attendant gives us a safety briefing, where he or she carefully demonstrates how an oxygen mask would drop from the compartment above our seats if needed. We are shown how to put the mask over our heads and get oxygen. Then, a word for those with a child. "Place the mask over your face first; then place it over your child's face." Since my son is now bigger than I am, he has offered to help me with mine in the event of an emergency.

Usually a parent would take care of a child's need first. But, in this case, Mom or Dad needs to breathe first or they won't be able to help their child breathe. In order to give a child breath, we first have to get some oxygen ourselves.

That "Mom and Dad first" approach is where spiritual reality begins, according to the Bible. You cannot give what you yourself do not have, and you cannot lead a child where you have not been. Having established this foundation, the Parenting Plan continues with a practical strategy for communicating God's truths:

Talk about them when you sit at home and when you walk
along the road, when you lie down and when you get up. . . .
Be careful that you do not forget the LORD." (Deuteronomy
6:7; 12)

In a few words, the way to make sure your kids are spiritually
ready is a *natural communication of a personal reality*.

The spiritual reality every child needs to find at home is, first
and foremost: *a relationship, not a religion*.

The reality is described in the biblical Parenting Plan as "love
the Lord your God." Love is a relationship word. A religion is not
a relationship, rules are not a relationship, and rituals are not a relationship. I am not married to Karen because I attend celebrations
of her special days or go to meetings she likes to go to or buy her
flowers. I am married to her on the basis of a lifetime love and a
lifetime commitment. A relationship with God is based on the
same kind of personal attachment and commitment.

This God-love we are to give our kids is not some syrupy,
celestial sentiment. It is love "with all your heart and with all your
soul and with all your strength." So much for spending an hour a
week in stained glass and hard pews, or paying your religious dues
with a few rituals, or saluting a creed. To have the spiritual reality
hole in their heart filled, our children need a Person, not a system!

A two-year-old boy showed me that in a way I have not forgotten. Kim, one of Lisa's five-year-old friends, had broken her leg.
To our two-year-old Doug, this was a tragedy as big as a major
earthquake would seem to us. He was so worried about it that
Karen stopped what she was doing and said, "Let's talk to Jesus
about Kim." Doug liked that idea, so they both prayed. Doug's
prayer was not quite as coherent as Karen's, but every bit as sincere,
"Jesus . . . Kim . . . help leg . . . amen."

A few minutes later, Doug was tugging on Karen's slacks as
she worked at the sink. "Mommy, pray for Kim." Maybe he
thought God had a short memory. In any case, they prayed for

Kim again and again and again, many times that afternoon. A couple of days later, Lisa came home from school with news that Kim's leg was not as badly broken as they first thought. She would be healed sooner than expected. Without a moment's hesitation, little Doug walked over to the kitchen wall and pointed at a picture of Jesus that was hanging there. Then, with a smile, he announced, "Jesus made Kim better." Now that was spiritual reality—a Person who loves us and whom we love.

Any census over the years would have recorded five people living at our house. But Karen and I counted six, and we wanted our kids to count one more, too. Like the other people in our home, we talk to this Person, seek his opinion through his Book, and watch him make a difference in our lives. This is not an imaginary playmate, but a real God who lives, not on a faraway cloud, but up close where we can love Him with all our heart.

The Parenting Plan makes "heart" an important issue. God says that His ways are "to be upon your hearts." Not in your head. Young people today have little interest in the God of religion or the God of a creed alone. They are relationship people, and a relationship is more than an affair of the head—it is an affair of the heart. Many children are left cold by the spiritual direction of their parents because it seems like too much of a head thing and not enough of a heart thing.

In fact, it is possible to come very close to a relationship with God, but miss it by eighteen inches—the distance from your head to your heart. The vital spiritual heritage God tells us to give our child is Someone in our heart.

For our child and for ourselves, spiritual reality is a relationship with God, not a religion about God. Secondly, spiritual reality is spontaneous, not official.

"IF HE'S LIKE YOU . . ."

Those airline flight attendants I mentioned earlier are rather predictable people. Somebody at the flight attendant factory wrote the script that almost all of them use faithfully. And those of us who fly a lot faithfully drift off. We probably should listen, but we've heard it all before. In the event of a sudden plague on the attendants, I believe I could do the takeoff and landing briefings.

But every once in a while, I get one who gets my attention.

Not long ago, my flight was brightened by an attendant with a sense of humor and the ability to be spontaneous. He made sure all the essential information was communicated, but it had life. "The captain has turned on the seat-belt sign, and we will be landing as soon as he can find the airport." Suddenly, I was tracking with this guy. "In preparation for landing, please put your seat in the upright and most uncomfortable position." I was all ears. He continued to keep us interested in his important information by giving it to us casually, not formally.

When the Ultimate Parenting Book describes how a parent can communicate spiritual reality, it suggests a similar approach:

> Talk about them when you sit at home and when you walk
> along the road, when you lie down and when you get up.
> (Deuteronomy 6:7)

In other words, when you have the most important information to communicate, do it naturally, informally, spontaneously. Children are a lot more likely to get the message if you transmit it in the classroom of everyday life—sitting at home, driving somewhere, at bedtime, at breakfast, at dinner. Spiritual reality is best communicated in real situations, not in formal presentations.

There are a lot of things a parent can delegate—cleaning the house, mowing the lawn, washing the car. We can delegate the teaching of algebra or soccer or piano. But the Creator makes it very clear that parents cannot delegate to others the spiritual equipping of their kids. "Bring them [your children] up in the training and instruction of the Lord" (Ephesians 6:4); that is the scriptural charge to parents.

The reason is simple—where else can they see God at work day after day if not at home? Home is reality, and spiritual reality is what they are starved for. A church or clergyman or book can show them the facts, but parents are divinely positioned to show them the reality.

Kids see God "with skin on" when Mom and Dad pray about a financial problem instead of panicking, when they show love to a hurting family with a practical act of kindness, when they forgive a child who just hurt them, when they often stop and give thanks for good things that happen, when they talk more about the blessings than the complaints. Our own children have heard a lot of words about love and compassion at our house. But they probably learned what the words meant the night we scoured the house for toys and clothes we could give to some burned-out families in a nearby city, or the time they organized the effort to collect clothes and food for our family to take to a cardboard village of homeless people in New York City. When the kids prayed for those people that night, they really prayed.

Many of the most personal spiritual realities are communicated when life provides those teachable moments. When one of our sons felt betrayed by a good friend, he and I had a great opportunity to chew on the biblical command to "not let the sun go down while you are still angry" (Ephesians 4:26). Our son pondered that for a few minutes, came back, and simply said, "Dad, five sunsets is enough." He learned the real-life lesson that day that harbored anger is not worth it.

Parents with their spiritual radar on look for these natural opportunities to make faith come alive in everyday situations. Something dirty they heard at school becomes a moment to teach the beauty of what is pure. A put-down at school that really hurt is a chance to teach where their worth really comes from and the courage it takes to not return evil for evil. Life is filled with teachable moments for a mom or dad who would seize them to make spiritual ideas take on flesh.

For years, we had an old, high-back blue chair in our living room. To most visitors it was just a "blue chair." But to the five of us, it was the "prayer chair." No, it did not glow or play organ music when you sat in it. It was just the place where each of us would sit at times when we needed the rest of the family to pray for us. The rest of us would gather round the prayer chair and pray for its occupant. I was there before some major trips or responsibilities. The kids were each there every year on the night before school started. We felt God was sitting there close many times.

But on other occasions, there was no time for the chair. Not when you're dashing out the door to a chemistry test or a game or a recital. So Karen or I would take just a moment at the back door to talk to the Sixth Family Member about the one who had the need.

Sometimes Karen and I have had to go over the kids' heads without their knowing. Often, one of the children has left us baffled, confused, anxious. We have seen them drifting toward a friend or a choice or an attitude that was mostly beyond our reach and our understanding. Time to go to the only perfect Father— the One who knows what we don't know about that child and goes where we can't go with that child.

We got caught a couple of times, even though the door was closed tight. When Doug and Lisa had that recent discussion about how "Mom and Dad raised us," they realized they had both blown our cover on separate occasions. Lisa explained, "We walked into your room quietly and saw you kneeling at the foot of the bed." Chances are, we were praying for them. There were a few situations where it would be more accurate to say we were fighting for them in God's presence. We have seen answers in different ways—sometimes God's obvious intervention, sometimes a new insight into a child as we asked God to help us see him or her through God's eyes, other times grace and patience to love and wait.

A friend called from Florida late one night and asked us what Bible verse we would like to have printed among sea shells on a sampler. We told her Isaiah 54:13. It has been in our hearts, and now on our wall, for years . . .

> All your children will be taught by the LORD,
> and great will be the peace of your children.

We have tried to teach our kids the Lord, and they absorbed some of the God-information we gave them. Our church did so much to nurture the seeds we tried to plant. But we knew that we had to show them the Lord at home, because ultimately the spiritual reality had to come from our classroom of everyday life.

It is that way for every child in every family. All the self-worth and satisfying love and stable authority in the world will not make up for a spiritual hole left unfilled in a child's heart. That is the void into which kids try to cram a chemical or a drink or a sexual partner. Or even success, friends, sports, activities—good things that still leave them empty, and sometimes dangerously depressed, because nothing has given them enough love, enough meaning, enough answers.

So, a parent has no more important mission than to naturally communicate the personal reality of a relationship with God. Karen summed up that reality with the cheery sendoff she has given our children each day as they left for school. It will always be on the tape in their hearts. "Have a nice day with Jesus!"

With Jesus. That is the reality we have wanted our kids to feel in our house, and then when they leave this house for a turbulent world. We can't go with them much anymore. He can.

I was deeply moved when I heard about a four-year-old boy who was dying of leukemia. His father visited him faithfully every night in the hospital. One night, as Dad was preparing to leave, the boy stopped him with a short, staggering question, "Daddy, what's God like?" His father was not ready for that one. He cleared his throat, licked his lips, and looked at the ceiling. Sensing Dad's uneasiness, the dying boy withdrew the question, "That's okay, Daddy." Then he added these simple, unforgettable words: "If He's like you . . . then I'm not afraid."

A dad. A mom. A child's bottom line on God.

12

Your Child,
Your Mirror

My sons think in puns, like me. My daughter pushes for a goal in any task, then gives herself a simple reward, like me. The first time our then future son-in-law Rick spent a week in our home, he observed our family's deep feelings on important issues. He commented to Lisa, "Every member of your family is a passionate person." Karen is. I am. And the three children are.

Actually, our kids are like two-legged mirrors, reflecting a lot of what is inside us. Sometimes the reflection is amusing, sometimes it's affirming, other times it's alarming. When parents look at their children, they ultimately find they are also looking at themselves.

Including their needs. As parents focus on the needs of their children, they open locked closets in their own lives. Inside are memories, hurts, struggles that might still be denied, if it were not for the mirror in the needs of a son or daughter. In pursuing our child's needs, we end up face-to-face with our own. We see the unfulfilled personal need for a sense of worth, of significance, of love without abandonment; the pain of the past; the wounded child inside the "together" adult; the secret darkness inside.

We discover what is hard to admit—that our well is not deep enough even to meet all our own needs, let alone the heart-needs of the child we love. Our own incompleteness keeps us from being the mom or dad we so desperately want to be.

Something is wrong inside our children. Something is wrong inside of us. It is because every family has cancer—spiritual cancer. When coach Pat Riley took over the New York Knicks, he saw the cancer in his players. One writer reported:

> Pat Riley said the Knicks had to patch up their differences
> and play as a team, or they would disintegrate as what Riley
> calls, the 'disease of me' drove them apart."[1]

The disease of me. That diagnosis sums up the cancer in every family—selfishness. My way, my view, my convenience, my schedule, my needs, my agenda, my expectations, my fulfillment—selfishness cancer that poisons mothers and fathers, daughters and sons. We have all been hurt by it, and we have all hurt others because of it. All too often, the ones we have hurt the most have been the ones we love the most, because of our seemingly incurable case of the disease of me. No wonder the middle letter of *sin* is "I."

Sin is a word that our generation has tried to retire. Yet every mother or father, every husband or wife, every son or daughter experiences its power and effects. Every parent was first a child, raised by imperfect parents. Then we became another generation of sin-crippled parents. Now, even as we do our best to be what our child needs, we keep stumbling over our "me-ness." Things we may have hated in our own parents, we end up reproducing in our children. As one mother confessed, "When I'm tired, I sound like my mother." Too often we say the things we thought we would never say, and do the things we thought we would never do.

Dr. Karl Menninger, the founder of American psychiatry, concluded that we may be trying to solve the symptoms rather than the real problem. In his book, *Whatever Became of Sin?*, he issued this challenge to our "modern" thinking:

> Is no one any longer guilty of anything? Guilty perhaps of a sin that could be repented and repaired or atoned for? . . . Anxiety and depression we all acknowledge, and even vague guilt feelings; but has no one committed any sins? Where, indeed, did sin go? What became of it?[2]

The reality revealed by the demands of parenting is that there is an animal inside us that wins all too often, at the expense of the people we love. If we could have beaten the darker side of us, we would have by now. Again and again, our sincere aspirations to be a better mother or father are sabotaged by the selfish, sinful side of us. Yet this very frustration, this admission that we are not enough, is the gateway to a powerful hope.

YOUR FAMILY'S GREATEST NEED OF ALL

When I was ten years old, I almost drowned. My friends and I were goofing off in Lake Michigan, and I was too proud to tell them I could not swim. That silence almost turned deadly when I lost my footing on a sudden drop-off. I panicked and swallowed so much of the lake that I could hardly yell "help." I remember waving an arm as I went under a second time.

Actually, it was as much my reputation as the lake that almost did me in. My friends saw me flailing, but they knew I was a clown and thought this was just part of the show. But I was losing it. To this day, I can still feel those awful feelings of helplessness and see that water burying me again.

Finally, someone took me seriously. Someone came to save me. When my rescuer reached for me, I knew what I needed to do. I didn't just yell, "Thanks for coming," or "You look strong!" I knew I could not save myself or contribute anything to the rescue. I grabbed the man who came to save me as if he were my only hope.

As I have looked at the needs of my children, at the unglued world they and I must somehow navigate, and at the disease of me in all of us, I have realized I was again in over my head. I need outside help to make it. Every honest parent I know is in the same overwhelmed position.

Suddenly a word we have shelved under "Religious" becomes a living, personal word. The word "Savior." We need what a drowning boy needed that day he could not rescue himself—the intervention of a strong Savior.

Face-to-face with our children's needs, we are face-to-face with our own. Confronting our own deep need, we stand face-to-face with Jesus Christ. The Rescuer. The Savior.

My wife knows I need a Savior. My children know I need a Savior. I cannot afford to miss him. No one can, because all of us are drowning spiritually. Sometimes it takes having a family to show us.

Your family's biggest problem is not financial pressure. It is not a difficult child or an impossible schedule or one parent trying to do everything. What your family needs most is a cure for the cancer of selfishness, for the disease of me, and a new mother or father. It's someone who looks and sounds just like you, but a parent changed on the inside by the only One who can.

It is that sin problem that is drowning us. God's Book makes clear that "we all, like sheep, have gone astray; each of us has turned to his own way" (Isaiah 53:6). The One we have left is the One who created us. We are away from God. And in case someone should object, "Not me!" God declares that "all have sinned and fall short of the glory of God" (Romans 3:23).

With a life full of pressures, being away from God does not initially seem to be our most urgent issue. But that is because our world does not understand what sin is and what it does.

A TRIP UP THE HILL

Sergei Krikalev wanted to come home from outer space. He was a cosmonaut for the Soviet Union when there still was a Soviet Union. His mission: a five-month orbit around the earth. So Sergei kissed his wife and little daughter good-bye in May of 1991 and told them he would see them in October.

Those next five months went well in space, but not so well on earth. There was revolution in Sergei's homeland, and by October the Soviet Union was coming apart. Unfortunately for a homesick cosmonaut, the space program was in chaos. They were not quite sure who was in charge anymore, so Sergei had to keep circling for another month, two months, five months! Finally, in May, the Russians launched a rescue. After ten long months, trapped in an orbit going nowhere, Sergei came home.

Occasionally most of us get that sense of being in an "orbit going nowhere." As the pilots and navigators of our children, we sometimes have difficulty answering their questions about life because we have so many of our own. In reality, we do have an orbit problem. When we begin to understand where we are compared to where we are supposed to be, we can see why sin is so devastating.

The orbit we were made for is explained by the only One who can tell us—the One who made us. Speaking of Jesus Christ, the Bible says, "All things were created by him and for him" (Colossians 1:16).

Created by Jesus . . . created for Jesus . . . we cannot find peace until we have Jesus.

But instead of living for Him, we have all chosen to live for us. This disease of me is ultimately a way of life that says, "God, you run the universe and I will run me." So we become cosmic rebels against the One who gave us life. Our anger, our chain-saw tongue, our lies, our sexual unfaithfulness in action or thought, our self-centeredness, our arrogance—so many attitudes and actions defy the ways God designed us to live. Angels obey Him, nature obeys Him, the galaxies obey Him, but we do things our way.

It is a good thing for the earth to revolve around the sun. The earth is where it was made to be, and it has warmth and light and life. But what if the earth were able to choose its orbit and decided, "I'd like to be in an orbit of my own, thank you"? Away from the sun with no warmth and no light, all life would cease.

In a sense, that is where we are because we have left God. We are created to revolve around our Creator, but we have chosen to go off on an orbit of our own. And now we are away from the only One who can give us the love and significance we have spent our whole lives looking for. The only One who can give us heaven when we die. The only One who can make us new fathers and mothers from the inside out.

Deep down inside us there is this haunting feeling that someday there will be a reckoning for this thing called sin. There will be. In the words of the only real Expert on eternity, "the wages of sin is death" (Romans 6:23). Not death as in stopping breathing, but death as in forever separation from the only One we cannot live without. The "me-living" of sin costs a man or woman the completeness they could have had on earth, and it costs a family the closeness they could have had if Mom or Dad could have gotten a cure. And ultimately, sin carries a death penalty. Forever.

So, like the stranded cosmonaut, every man and woman is trapped in an orbit going nowhere. But a rescue mission was launched, and by the very One we have defied. The Rescuer? God's only Son, Jesus. On a hill outside of Jerusalem, the rescue was accomplished when Jesus Christ paid the death penalty each of us deserves. It is the central message of the Bible that "Christ died for sins once for all, the righteous [that's Jesus] for the unrighteous [that's us] to bring you to God" (1 Peter 3:18).

In the greatest act of love any of us could ever imagine, God's Son paid our sin-bill. We did the sinning . . . Jesus did the dying. This opens the way for meeting the deepest need of the human heart—a personal relationship with the God we were made by and made for.

The Rescuer, the Savior has come to save us from the sin and selfishness from which we could never save ourselves. But that does not guarantee we will not drown. As I learned that nearly fatal day in Lake Michigan, you have to grab the rescuer. If you do not trust him to save you, you die, even though he put his life on the line to rescue you.

Trust is the difference between living and dying spiritually. God explains how a person can trade a death penalty for eternal life: "For God so loved the world that he gave his one and only Son, that whoever believes in him shall not perish but have eternal life" (John 3:16).

When God says "believe in him [Jesus]," He is talking about something you do with your heart, not just with agreement in your head. "For it is with your heart that you believe. . . . everyone who calls on the name of the Lord will be saved" (Romans 10:10, 13). In other words, you stop dying and start living the moment you pin all your hopes on Jesus Christ—just as a drowning person would grab a lifeguard and say, "You are my only hope."

In a sense, you have to make a trip up the hill with the cross of Jesus at the top. And there, at the foot of his cross, you kneel and talk to him in words something like these: "Lord, I've been running my life, and now I realize how wrong that is. You made me for you, and I've stubbornly lived for me. I'm sorry for all my sin and selfishness. I want to be forgiven, Lord, and I want you to change me. I need a Savior. I believe some of those sins you are dying for here are mine. And right now, I am pinning all my hopes on you to have my sins erased from God's book, to make a new beginning for me and my family, and to have eternal life. Jesus, beginning this day, I am yours."

Forgiveness for all the failures. The hole in your heart finally filled. Judgment canceled. A love you will never lose and that will never lose you. All because you have acknowledged your need for the Savior, and trusted in His rescuing power.

That power won for good three days after Jesus was on that cross. Jesus Christ walked out of his grave under his own power, conquering the power that has beaten every person but Him—death. This is a living Savior to whom you commit your life. From the moment you know Jesus, He can enter your family—through you. And He can change everything. Starting with you.

A NEW BEGINNING FOR THE PEOPLE YOU LOVE

"If anyone is in Christ, he is a new creation; the old has gone, the new has come!" (2 Corinthians 5:17). That guarantee from God Himself is the anchor of a powerful hope for a home. We don't have to be what we have been, or what our parents were. We can begin to be new because of the transforming presence of Jesus Christ in the control room of our life.

Our lifelong journey for the missing part of us is over. That journey wound through our own childhood, through disappointing relationships, through busy years that filled our calendar but not our heart, through loneliness that persisted in a crowd or even in someone's arms, and then to the time a precious child joined us on our journey—and finally to life's ultimate challenge—trying to be all that child needs us to be.

There, in the "child mirror" before us, we have seen our own deep need, and come to the Savior we have been looking for all along.

❈　❈　❈

Dad and Scotty had different agendas for the night Mom was out. Dad was going to read his newspaper and drift into nap-land. Scotty was going to play hide-and-seek with his Daddy. He had been put off several times, so he finally asked pitifully, "Are you ever going to have time to play with me?" With the sports page, the cartoons, and the nap still undone, Dad was looking for something to buy a little more time. That was when he noticed the next page of the newspaper—a whole-page map of the entire world!

"You like puzzles, right, Scotty?" he asked, tearing the page into pieces. Scotty gave a tentative yes as his father handed him a handful of pieces. "As soon as you put that map together, I'll play," Dad explained. Scotty was not thrilled. But Dad vanished into the news of last night's game as his son went to work on the floor.

Only two minutes later Scotty pushed through the sports page into his father's lap. "I got it!" the little boy declared.

"Already?" Dad said. "That was a picture of the whole world!"

"There was a picture of a man on the other side, Daddy," Scotty explained. "And when you put the man together right, the world goes together just fine!"

Yes, it does. Jesus Christ is in the business of putting mothers together, and fathers together, and then, children. When we allow the Savior to put us together, our world and our family go together just fine.

Then we can make a grandmother's precious prayer our own. As she told me about her family, she told me about the prayer she has kept on her bedroom wall all these years. I have not been able to get it out of my heart.

> *It is my greatest prayer*
> *That on that Resurrection Day*
> *I may stand before my Savior and say,*
> *"Here am I . . . and the children you gave me."*

Addendum:

A Special Word for Single Parents

I n southern California, they have earthquakes. Some years ago a friend of mine from that area told me about a seldom-mentioned effect of those quakes.

He told me that a university's Trauma Counseling Center had suddenly been inundated with children after a recent earthquake. The center had relatively few children as clients, until southern California started shaking. "The children were traumatized," the one counselor explained. "Everything that had never moved before suddenly started moving. Children were devastated."

Everything that had never moved before suddenly started moving. That trauma not only describes what happens to children when the earth shakes, it also describes when a family is shaken, too, by the effects of divorce or death.

The effect of a family-quake on a child can be devastating. Left with the challenge of providing some stability is a now-single parent who has himself or herself been deeply shaken. This person is no longer a husband or wife, but the responsibility of parenting has not changed. Except, possibly, to become more intense.

So, as we have pursued meeting a child's heart-needs, a single parent may want to raise a hand and inquire, "What about me? This is challenging for two parents, so how do I do it alone?"

Important questions. Questions that deserve a brief detour from the main road of those five needs.

No, there is no separate parenting strategy for single parents. A child's needs for resources such as a secure self, sexual answers, and satisfying love do not change because there is only one parent. The basic agenda of meeting the needs behind the deeds should be the mission of every parent. In fact, this emphasis on the *why* more than the *what* of a child's behavior can help focus a single parent's limited energies.

There is no doubt that a solo mom or dad is under extreme pressure after the "quake." Bleeding from their own wounds, fighting for their own economic and emotional survival, struggling to find their own solo identity—single parents have a lot to handle without a child's needs. Yet those needs won't go away. If they are neglected, the heartbreak of a death or divorce may one day be compounded by the heartbreak of a shipwrecked child.

Any answers for single parents are in danger of sounding pat or trite: "It's easy for you to say." Still, there is no separate truth for single parents. Certain eternal principles actually become more important when your partner is gone. Although every family is unique, we must take the risk of applying these principles to the pain, the pressures, and the potential of a one-parent home.

There actually may be healing in focusing on a child's needs instead of mainly focusing on one's own. Rather than the child's heart-needs being "one more thing to do," they can become the larger focus that helps lift a parent out of his or her pit.

For every single parent there are potential hurt factors and potential hope factors in the parent-child challenge. The hurt factors increase the trauma and pain for parent and child, both already scarred by the divorce or death. The hope factors, on the other hand, create an attitude and a climate which can provide stability for both parent and child. If we can identify those factors, then a single parent can fight the hurt factors and focus on the hope factors.

HURT FACTOR # 1: THE CHAIN OF BITTERNESS

Author Philip Yancey tells a story that graphically illustrates the destructive power of bitterness, the first of the hurt factors.

"I have a friend whose marriage has gone through rough times. One night George passed a breaking point and emotionally exploded. He pounded the table and floor. 'I hate you!' he screamed at his wife. 'I won't take it anymore! I've had enough! I won't go on! I won't let it happen! No! No! No!' Several months later, my friend woke up in the middle of the night and heard strange sounds coming from the room where his two-year-old son slept. He went down the hall, stood outside his son's door, and shivers ran through his flesh. In a soft voice, the two-year-old son was repeating word for word with precise inflection the climactic argument between his mother and father. 'I hate you . . . I won't take it anymore . . . No! No! No!'"[1]

Then Yancey forcefully concludes: "George realized that in some awful way he had just passed on his pain and anger and unforgiveness to the next generation."

That dark legacy of anger and unforgiveness is a danger for any single mom or dad. Especially when there has been a divorce, there is often a cancerous bitterness left behind. Ironically, bitterness is the longest chain in the world. It chains the embittered person to the one he or she resents. When you carry a grudge, you carry the person against whom you have the grudge. You are tied emotionally to the very individual you do not want to be near. The unforgiven person is there in your decisions, your conversations, your plans, your thoughts, your dreams, and you can't stop thinking about him or her!

For the divorced parent, of course, the great danger is that your son or daughter will be infected with this emotional killer. For one thing, it is tempting to try to turn a child against the one who hurt you. It seems to provide perverse comfort and vindication if you can get your son or daughter to adopt your condemnation of your former partner.

In other cases, the grudge-transfer is unintentional. Like George's son in Yancey's account, the bitterness is caught, not taught. In either case, the child is cursed with a hand-me-down hatred that will infect many life relationships.

If anyone ever needed the grace of God, it is a single parent. That is why the Bible's warning is so arresting: "See to it that no one misses the grace of God and . . . [this is how it happens] that no bitter root grows up to cause trouble and defile many" (Hebrews 12:15). God's grace and our bitterness cannot coexist in the same heart—one or the other has to go!

The pain of a divorce and the pressures of single parenting, for both parent and child, are bad enough. Facing them without God's grace is just too much. Yet many single parents do just that, because they are carrying the ugliness of the past into the present by letting bitterness have a room in their hearts, and thereby "defiling" (that's the Bible's word) their child's heart, too.

When divorced parents pump anti-other-parent input into a child's heart, they are encouraging that child to divorce a mother or father. And that puts a son or daughter in direct violation of one of the Ten Commandments, "Honor your father and mother." Notice, it does not say "your father *or* mother." And the commandment does not say, "if they are honorable." Neither a divorce nor a dishonorable parent changes a child's responsibility to both parents.

Bitterness simply compounds, deepens, and preserves the pain. It is, indeed, the longest emotional chain in the world. There is only one way to break the chain—forgiveness. Not a warm feel-

ing. Not a denial of the hurt or the sins of the hurter. A choice—
forgiveness is a choice.

Why choose it? Because forgiving is right (even if it is hard).
Because forgiving is healing. Because forgiving cuts the chain and
lets you and your son or daughter get on with your lives. And
because bitterness is just too expensive. Everything in us cries out,
"No! It isn't fair! I deserve to harbor this! I need to hate this person!" But that unforgiver in our soul is only prolonging the pain
and wounding others. The day we choose to stop hating and hurting and harboring is the beginning of emotional freedom.

There is only one problem—I'm not sure we can forgive one
who has deeply wounded us without the resources of the Great
Forgiver. He is the One who prayed for those who executed him,
"Father, forgive them" (Luke 23:34). We may be able to choose to
forgive the person who hurt us, but we need something supernat-
ural in our heart to really let it happen.

We will continue to need those divine resources because forgiving is more of a process than an event. It begins when a person
makes the choice, then cries out to Jesus, the Forgiver, "I can't. I'm
not even sure I want to. But I'm opening up to you for forgivabil-
ity only you can give me."

Whatever it takes, the chain of bitterness must be broken.
There has been enough hurt for a parent and a child. It is time to
file the pain of the past and declare a new beginning.

HURT FACTOR # 2: THE MONSTER OF "ME"

"Come on, Daddy, read 'Winnie the Pooh'!" That was a frequent cry in our family's "bedtime story era." The kids would
come in their jammies-with-feet, carrying the "Pooh" book opened
to the page where we had left off.

I'm not sure if the appeal was the story, the laptime, or the
weird voices. I cannot read a story in a normal way. I have this

assortment of strange voices with which I try to make each character come to life. So, Piglet came out high and nasal; Pooh was dreamy-sounding with words exploding from puffed-out cheeks; and Eeyore, the donkey, was slow and pokey. Eeyore got the most laughs.

That was ironic because Eeyore was never very happy. He was the "poor me" member of the cast, always worrying or complaining, usually feeling sorry for himself.

A four-legged Eeyore in a story may be amusing. A two-legged "Eeyore" in real life is not. That is what some people have become through the death of a marriage or a mate. The monster of "me" can add another hurt factor to a vulnerable single-parent family. A mom or dad alone has to fight the encroachment of some sinister "self" words.

For example, look at self-pity. The burdens of single parenting are real and heavy, but they don't get any lighter by complaining about them. In fact, they become heavier as you "psyche yourself out" by talking about them. In addition, "Eeyore complaining" further erodes the stability a single-parented child needs more than ever. Instead of a parent carrying a child on his or her back, the child ends up carrying the whining, guilt-tripping parent. That is backwards, and it will end up crushing them both.

It might be interesting to tape your home conversations for one day and note the number of times you give off self-pitying complaints. "I have so much to do. I have so little help. I've been through so much. I get so little thanks." The monster of me does not produce a very inspiring script.

Self-focus is another me monster. That "self" word grows rapidly in the soil of single-parent survival. When you are left alone, by either death or divorce, you automatically start thinking survival. Survivalism usually says, "There's nobody looking out for me now. If I don't look out for me, no one else will." That kind of thinking can cause an emotional moat to develop between a parent and a child. A son or daughter picks up many signals that seem to say, "Don't bother me, kid. Don't you realize what I'm up against here? Sorry about your needs; I've got huge needs of my own right now. Maybe later."

And children get the message. Most will back off, feeling guilty about bothering you, the self-focused parent. But their needs will still be crying inside them, and the irretrievable days will continue to fly by. They will then take the needs that were supposed to be met at home to someone else. And suddenly a child is a disaster looking for a place to happen.

Are self-pity and self-focus natural feelings for a struggling single parent? Usually. Are they helpful in the healing and stabilizing process? Not at all. The monster of me is a hurt factor in a single-parent family. And monsters should be eliminated, not tolerated.

HURT FACTOR # 3: THE AVALANCHE OF EXPECTATIONS

Single parents could use a Saint Bernard to rescue them from the avalanche that hits when "it's all up to me now." Buried in expectations usually carried by two people, they sometimes are starved for oxygen.

The tendency is to bury your children in an avalanche of expectations—especially emotional expectations. Feeling alone, single parents may inadvertently expect their son or daughter to be their best friend, primary emotional support, and even substitute mate. When a single parent emotionally "marries" a child, they both get hurt. The parent will inevitably be hurt and disappointed by a child who was never meant to be so depended upon. In fact, the need-meeting agenda gets inverted as a parent says to a child, "Your job is to meet my needs." Wasn't it supposed to be the other way around? The child will inevitably be hurt by being robbed of a childhood and of a nurturing parent.

More hurt is the last thing a single-parent family needs. That is why an effective single parent recognizes the hurt factors and fights them—the chain of bitterness, the monster of me, and the avalanche of expectations. They may come naturally, but they cost too much.

What this wounded family needs is some hope!

HOPE FACTOR # 1: RECYCLING THE GARBAGE

Recycling is a pain, but it's a good idea. I guess the alternative is a growing synthetic glacier, steadily creeping in our direction. Something has to be done with all the bottles and cans!

In our town, that means we get to go out late one night a month and sort our glass, plastic, and newspapers. We get to carry all those receptacles out to the street, where the Recycling Fairy makes them disappear, usually with lots of noise before we planned to be awake.

Like I said, though, it is a good idea. I am amazed how environmental experts can take my Coke bottle or can—garbage to me—and remake it into something useful. Or how they can take our trash and recycle it into landfill on which hotels, condos, and airports can be built.

In a sense, positive single parents are in the recycling business, too. Yes, there is garbage from the divorce or the death. In themselves, these tragedies are only ugly. But from the garbage something useful can come.

If single parents need to fight the hurt factors, they need to focus on the hope factors. Certainly, that includes emotional recycling that focuses not on the garbage, but on the good that can come from it.

For example, one positive result of emotional recycling is strong character. Many children in single-parent families are forced to grow up more quickly than their peers. The growth comes from being forced to take responsibility while many of their peers are postponing responsibility as long as they can. While a young person should not be burdened with all the parent's pressures, they can be more actively involved in family decision-making than others their age would be. And, if single-parent children are nurtured in this direction, they can take life a little more seriously because of the reality shocks they have been forced to process.

All those traits can form the character of a leader. No one would have wished for the pain that gives birth to maturity. But a wise single parent focuses a child on the character that the "garbage" can produce.

Strong bonds are also a plus that can come out of a minus. Crisis forces people together. And the demands on a family with a missing parent are often critical. Those pressures can create conflict if parent and child allow themselves to turn on each other. Or they can forge a combat-deepened closeness that nothing can break—a closeness that might not have happened without the tragedy.

Strong lessons can also be recycled from the garbage, especially where there has been a divorce. On the one hand, a single parent should not create bitterness by reciting all the ugliness in the other parent. But it is constructive to review what went wrong. A son or daughter can make better choices and build a stronger future if he or she can learn the lessons of a broken marriage. How to choose a mate, the importance of waiting, the discipline of dealing with problems when they are small, the necessity of time and communication, these lessons can be powerful against the backdrop of the consequences of not learning them.

Also, pain and desperation are often recycled into strong faith. The death of a marriage or a mate can emotionally bankrupt a person. It is in those hopeless, helpless times that we can learn to collapse in God's arms. That is when a person discovers a power he never knew existed.

I saw that happen to Wendy. Her husband, my friend, died at the age of thirty-three, leaving her with three unfinished children. Bill had been a strong husband, and there was much Wendy was not prepared to take over. I walked into the funeral home that cold night, trying to think of how I might comfort her. There she stood by Bill's steel-gray casket, arms around her three fatherless children. I didn't have to say much—Wendy was encouraging us. She was miraculously okay. Gently but confidently, she whispered three words, "Jesus is enough."

There is no way to know that Jesus is all you need until Jesus is all you've got. And in her moment of deepest pain, Wendy had cried out to God and found resources she had never fully known before, because she had never needed them so desperately.

Positive parents can, with their children, discover treasure in their tragedy, the "unloseable," inexhaustible love and power of God. As long as we can trust in anyone or anything else, we usually will. But single parenting can bring us to an emotional poverty that drives us to the Bank of Heaven. There a parent and child can find spiritual wealth they would never have discovered without the pain.

Strong character, strong bonds, strong lessons, and strong faith are the valuables a single parent can recycle out of the garbage of brokenness. Some may look at the bottles and cans set out by our street and say, "Trash." But the recycler looks at it and says, "Trash today, treasure tomorrow. Ugly today, useful tomorrow." The recycling single parent looks at the garbage and determines to turn it into gold.

HOPE FACTOR # 2: ACKNOWLEDGING YOUR LIMITATIONS

It can be discouraging. You're a single parent, and you know the things you need to do for your son or daughter. You need to be there when your kids come and go from school, be at their events, be available when they need to talk, and be together for meals. You need to and you want to, but sometimes you can't.

You have to work to keep the family financially alive. When that work ends, the laundry and checks and errands begin. Frankly, there is a limit to your time and your energy. The gap between "want to" and "able to" creates guilt, frustration, and worry.

Even these limitations can be captured and made into a hope factor. The children of single parents need to know how much Mom or Dad wants to be there and why she or he can't. Rather than suffering quietly in this case, single parents can let their kids know where their heart is, even if their body cannot be there. The next best thing to your being there is letting your child know how much you want to be there. It helps to explain how what you're doing instead is also for them.

Most children can understand their parent's limitations if they are explained. Then they can adjust their expectations rather than being disappointed at the last minute. If a child knows when a parent is available, he or she can usually deal with the unavailable times. Every time you, as a parent, can adjust some responsibilities to be there when you usually are tied up, let it be a special surprise. Because you have explained your limitations, it will mean a lot when you sacrificially go beyond those limitations for the love of a child. Also, if you have to be missing at a major moment, you may be able to arrange for someone to video or photograph it. Later, your son or daughter can be your personal commentator as you make it to their moment through pictures. If the moment missed is not photo-capturable, you can ask for a blow-by-blow account at your first opportunity.

When single parents go the extra mile to explain, circumvent, and compensate for their limitations, these negatives can have a positive effect: "I know this is really hard for my mom, but she is really going above and beyond to make up for it." I think that's called "feeling loved."

HOPE FACTOR # 3: BALANCING THE LOSSES

In order for single parents to focus on the third hope factor, they need a lesson in emotional math. Every time you subtract one, you add one, leaving you even. That is called balancing the losses a child may experience because of the limitations on a single parent. In other words, for every negative, a single parent needs to give a son or daughter a compensating positive.

"I can't be with you on Tuesday night, but Saturday morning is all yours for whatever you want to do together." It's that kind of compensation thinking that creates a credit to balance each debit in a parent-child account.

Over the years, I have traveled quite a bit in my work. Often, I have seen the disappointment in a child's eyes because I was going to be gone. I chased some pretty crazy flight schedules to make it back for a recital or Sunday dinner, but there were still times when my absence was felt. Minus one in the father-son or father-daughter account.

In times like those, I found myself asking, "What can I do with them that will compensate for my absence?" Some of the answers to my question sounded like this: "As soon as I get home, we'll have a family game of baseball," "We'll go out to eat and you'll pick the place," "We'll go to the baseball card show," or "We'll go away for the weekend." Suddenly, my absence didn't seem like such a bad idea—not if it could be traded for a "goodie."

For twenty years, I knew this was a tightrope walk, with no way to measure if being present was balanced against being absent, and if being totally available was compensating in their parent-love accounts for being unavailable other times.

I did not get a debit-credit statement on those accounts until recently. One of my now grown-up sons settled down in a chair in my study and gave me the report. He had been asked in a college class what he remembered about his relationship with his father.

"Two things," he told them and now reported to me. "First, my father was gone a lot." My heart sank. "Absent" had won. "Secondly, I had my father a lot." I looked down at my desk and whispered, "Thank you, God." By his grace, the pluses and the minuses had balanced—and my son knew how much he mattered to me.

We had tried to capture every moment together we could, whether a trip to the gas station, the grocery store, or an opportunity to take him to or from school. I guess my goal had been that each child know one thing about my time with him or her: "If I possibly can be with you, I will be."

That is the message parents send when they consciously balance their absences with their presences, their "can'ts" with their "cans," and their no's with their yeses. In that kind of atmosphere, children know they are loved and desirable and valuable.

An effective single parent is an emotional accountant, taking every possible opportunity to make another love-deposit in the heart of a child.

HOPE FACTOR # 4: COUNTING ON REINFORCEMENTS

In the old Westerns, the climactic scene would often find the wagons in a circle, waiting for the Indians' final attack. Wagons were burning, guns were almost empty, and the only people still alive were the ones whose name had been in big print at the beginning of the movie. The small-print names were expendable.

Then, just as the Indians began to swoop down for the kill, you would hear the inevitable bugle. Yes! Over the hill at full gallop came the cavalry, the boys in blue! There are many days when a single parent feels like those beleaguered settlers, and the wagons are in a circle. With an arrow through the hat and an empty rifle, this parent feels those "last roundup" feelings. "One parent just isn't enough," he or she sighs. "There's just not enough of me. I'm running on empty." It's time for reinforcements.

It is easy for a single parent to live in a survival mode, and a survival mentality often causes a person to retreat into a self-focused, isolated shell. Ironically, this "I've got to make it alone now" way of thinking robs a parent of the very resources he or she needs to survive. Someone raising a child alone can ill afford to let pain or pride keep them from reaching out to other people. While no one person can take the place of a missing father or mother, a network of friends, family members, and church friends can go a long way in making up the difference.

There are a lot of resources available for one who is willing to use that powerful four-letter word, "Help." Often there is a family member or friend who needs to be needed, and a single parent's call could help them as well as you.

One of the great God-given resources for family deficits is the "family" of a church. Even with two parents, our own children have benefited from unofficial "aunts," "uncles," and "grandparents" in our church who have "adopted" them.

It is probably unfair to expect too much of any one outside helper. Their help can rapidly disappear if the burdens they are asked to share are too many. That's why it is important to seek out several support people, each of whom could relieve a little of the pressure—a chauffeuring need, helping with difficult homework, taking a child on a special outing that the missing parent would usually do, attending an event the child is a part of, providing opportunities to earn money, etc.

The pressures of single parenting can seem insurmountable, even with a network of caring people around you. There is Someone who wants to be the difference in this seemingly impossible equation. He demonstrated that many times when he visited our planet. In one poignant incident, Jesus Christ was inching His way through a wall-to-wall crowd. Buried in that throng was a desperate woman with a disease no doctor had been able to cure for twelve years. Now she was out of doctors, out of money, out of hope. The wagons were in a circle.

But Jesus was in town. With dogged determination, she pushed her way through that mob, muttering to herself, "If I can just get to Jesus, if I can just get to Jesus . . ." And she did. Almost out of hope, she lunged for her last hope, and touched his robe in one desperate act of faith. She was, in the words of the biblical record, "immediately . . . freed from her suffering" (Mark 5:29). The reinforcements had made the difference—reinforcements from heaven itself.

Jesus' disciples were amazed when their Lord asked, "Who touched me?" Hundreds were trying to touch Him, but He knew one person out of that faceless multitude had lunged for Him in powerlessness and faith. The biblical historian records this revealing footnote: "She could not go unnoticed" (Luke 8:47).

Desperate people can never go unnoticed—not in the eyes of Jesus.

On the days when you, as a single parent, have nothing left to give, you do not go unnoticed. You only need to reach, even lunge, for the Lord of the desperate.

He is the God who does a strange and wonderful miracle when a human being loses a kidney. Suddenly, the body's kidney capacity is cut in half. That is when that single overworked kidney begins to experience the Creator's touch. It starts to grow—until its capacity has doubled! God enlarges that single organ until it can miraculously do the work it once took two to do!

The God who can do that for single kidneys can certainly do that for single parents. If you face the challenges of your children largely alone, you can reach out to the Lord who gives one the grace and love and strength of two. Only he can enlarge a single parent and enable him or her to do the work that would normally be done by two.

The demands of parenting and the needs of your children are manageable. This battle can be won, but not alone. "If I can just get to Jesus"—He was the answer for one woman without hope, and He can be the answer for you.

In a sense, you don't ever have to be a single parent again. Once you have come to Him by faith, He will never let you be alone again.

Notes

Chapter 1— *The Key That Unlocks Parenting*

1. Neil Postman, *The Disappearance of Childhood* (New York: Delacorte Press, 1982).

Chapter 4— *Taming the Birds and Bees*

1. Letters to the Editor, *Newsweek* (December 28, 1992): 16.

Chapter 7— *Six Secrets of Love Your Child Can Feel*

1. Arlene Levinson, Associated Press editorial, *The Record* (Hackensasck, N.J.) (December 27, 1992).

Chapter 11— *No Unguided Missiles*

1. Lyric excerpts from "Sunrise, Sunset." Lyrics by Sheldon Harnick, music by Jerry Bock. Copyright © 1964 by Alley Music Corp. and Trio Music Co., Inc. Copyright renewed and assigned to Mayerling Productions Ltd. (admin. in the U.S. by R&H Music Co.) and Jerry Bock Enterprises for the United States and to Alley Music Corp., Trio Music Co., Inc., and Jerry Bock Enterprises for the world outside the United States. Used by permission. All rights reserved.

Chapter 12— *Your Child, Your Mirror*

1. Chris Smith, "The Knicks Go for the Grand Slam," *New York* (May 31, 1993): 35.

2. Karl Menninger, *Whatever Became of Sin?* (New York: Hawthorn Books, 1973), 133.

Addendum— *A Special Word for Single Parents*

1. Philip Yancey, "Holocaust & Ethnic Cleansing," *Christianity Today*, (August 16, 1993): 28.

If you would like to know more about a personal relationship with Jesus Christ, I would love to hear from you. The address is:

Ron Hutchcraft Ministries
P.O. Box 1818
Wayne, NJ 07474-1818

If you would like more information about the work and resources of Ron Hutchcraft Ministries, you may contact us at the same address.

Ron Hutchcraft

———————

Ron Hutchcraft is an author, speaker, and radio host. A thirty-year veteran of student and family work, Ron has spoken around the world to thousands of young people, parents, leaders, and professional athletes, presenting practical answers to real-life issues.

Mr. Hutchcraft hosts several international radio programs, including the popular daily broadcast "A Word with You," the parent-equipper "Threshold," and the youth program "Alive! with Ron Hutchcraft." He is also the author of *Peaceful Living in a Stressful World*, *Wake-Up Calls*, and *Letters from the College Front*, guys' edition and girls' edition.